Play All

Clive James

Play All

A BINGEWATCHER'S NOTEBOOK

Yale

UNIVERSITY PRESS

New Haven and London

Yale University Press books may be purchased in quantity for
educational, business, or promotional use. For information, please
e-mail sales.press@yale.edu (U.S. office) or sales@yaleup.co.uk
(U.K. office).

Designed by Sonia L. Shannon.
Set in Fournier type by Integrated Publishing Solutions.
Printed in the United States of America.

Library of Congress Control Number: 2016930355
ISBN 978-0-300-21809-1 (hardcover : alk. paper)

A catalogue record for this book is available from the British
Library.

This paper meets the requirements of ANSI/NISO Z39.48-1992
(Permanence of Paper).

10 9 8 7 6 5 4 3 2 1

To Prue, Lucinda, and Claerwen
WATCHERS OF THE AVALANCHE

And to Farran Nehme, Alice Gregory, and Meghan O'Rourke
KIDS FROM BROOKLYN

And to Marina Hyde, Hadley Freeman, Catherine Shoard, and Zoe Williams
SHAKERS OF THE SUPERFLUX

And to Simon Schama and Jonathan Meades
KINGS OF THE WALKING TALK

And to James Gandolfini and Philip French
GHOSTS AT THE FEAST

And to Jonny Grove, Maia Grove, and Benjamin Beresford
IMAGE CONSULTANTS

And to Steven Bochco, Carl Reiner, Richard Benjamin, and Peter Bogdanovich
PRINCIPAL ELDERS

Und doch darf ich nicht klagen. Es tut so wohl noch einmal Ja zu sagen.

—KURT TUCHOLSKY

And yet I mustn't complain. It's so good to say "Yes" for once.

Contents

Acknowledgments

FOR CRITICAL ADVICE on my text, I should thank Claerwen James, Lucinda James, Deirdre Serjeantson, and David Free. The opinions are still my own, but some of them have become less intransigent through having been hauled over the coals.

A Note on the Text

APART FROM A FEW PARAGRAPHS of a piece about *Mad Men* which first appeared in the *Weekend Australian Review* in 2009, and perhaps a few opinions from a piece about *The Pacific* that appeared in the *Times Literary Supplement* in 2010, everything in this book was written in these recent years of my illness, while it went on happily refraining from being fatal. With memories in my head of how *Twin Peaks* had once held my attention with its long story even though I could barely understand its briefest episode, I sat down with my younger daughter Lucinda to watch a big box of *NYPD Blue* right through. We had seen it all before, but as in a glass, darkly. Our recurring discussion of the magnificence of Andy Sipowicz set a tone that struck me with its potential for one day becoming a useful critical style. This tone was abetted by reports of water-cooler conversations that Lucinda brought home from her work as a civil servant, and from dinner table conversations in my elder daughter Claerwen's kitchen, where I found myself matching her admiration for Starbuck in *Battlestar Galactica* with mine for Wilma Deering in *Buck Rogers in the 25th Century*. It occurred to me, perhaps because of my medicated state, that a new critical language was developing itself to deal with the onrush of creativity coming to us in the form of box sets: a system of distribution that still strikes me as something new, even though it is already being overtaken by systems that download material directly into the computer. By the time this book is published, the DVD might be as obsolete as the dodo. But the number of shows, if not their quality, can only go on increasing: and the way we talk about them can only become more compulsively attentive than it was a few years back, when I first noticed that Allison Janney in *The West Wing* was getting the kind of detailed analytical praise that Maria Callas used to get when she sang in *Tosca* at Covent Garden. I could hear the same fluent critical inventiveness from the discussion groups of writers on *Slate* when they talked about the first few episodes of *Orange Is the New Black:* some of the writers sounded as if they were having at least as much fun talking as they did writing.

Since I have always thought that the spontaneous response of the delighted consumer outranks the more ponderous consideration of the professional student of culture, I took this to be a welcome development, and tried to hang on to the sense of irresponsibility when I sat down to write. Though my tone is conversational, however, I have tried as always to stick to the fixed grammatical rules on which free expression depends, and I would have written "boxed sets" for "box sets" if the neologism had not already become standard. Back in the eighteenth century, I might have agreed with Swift that the word "idololatry" was etymologically correct and that "idolatry" was a barbarism to be staved off at all costs. We would have lost, however: and today there is a good reason for at least acknowledging popular usage when talking about popular culture. Not to do so sounds too aloof. Sometimes the subject is grim, but we wouldn't even be discussing it if its presentation were not entertaining. When Deirdre Serjeantson gave me a box set of *Veronica Mars* for Christmas, I wondered briefly what Theodor Adorno would have said on the subject of American schoolgirl detectives, but after watching a few episodes I realized that I didn't give a damn what Theodor Adorno would have said: I only wanted to see more of what Kristen Bell was doing with the title role. Through-out the text, I have taken care to name the actors, who should always, I think, be given at least that much reward for their work. All too often we think of them as having chosen their roles. They hardly ever get that chance. In that regard we viewers live in a dream world, being guided toward reason by people who live in a world of harsh reality.

—Cambridge, 2016

Play All

Title Sequence

IT SEEMS AN AGE AGO NOW, and it was. Between 1972 and 1982 I wrote a regular weekly column about television for the London *Observer,* and by the end of my stint I preened myself as being fairly clued up on the subject. I signed off with a confident prediction that although the American production centers, having fed their shows to the networks, might go on picking up secondary earnings by flooding the world with stuff priced low because it had already made a profit in the home market, the droll sarcasm of the desk sergeant Phil Esterhaus (Michael Conrad) in *Hill Street Blues* would be about as clever as their effort would ever get. Seriousness, sophistication, and the thrill of creativity could be supplied only by the older, wiser, more mature nations. For a couple of decades it looked as if I might be right, and then the American cable channels, arising out of nowhere, suddenly outflanked the networks, which, in their turn, were obliged to raise their game. American shows for export increased their status from merely ubiquitous to unbeatably attractive, and then the advent of the box set dramas changed the game completely, to the extent that the old world had to start competing or be left out.

But to compete was hard: the American product was so good. This unexpected upsurge was a replay, in the form of art, of what the Americans had done in World War II, for which, at the beginning, they had very little military equipment, and by the end, after only a few short years, they were building a new aircraft carrier every fortnight and had developed the B-29 pressurized high-altitude bomber, not to mention the atomic bomb. None of that had been predictable either, but the thought did not console me when, at the millennium, I looked back on my confident pronouncements of the early 1980s and lashed myself for having so completely failed to guess what might happen to the American television output later on. It was a punishing example of what ought to be a critical rule: if you can't quell your urge to make predictions, don't make them about the future.

As I begin composing this short treatise about binge-watching and the general cultural importance of the box set TV show, I have just watched, for the third time, the episode of *The Good Wife* in which Will (spoiler alert!) solves the ethical problems arising from his love affair with Alicia by getting himself shot. I forbear from specifying whether his wound is fatal. I merely say that he ends up feeling even more wiped out than I do. Since my polite but insidious form of leukemia was diagnosed in early 2010, it has been more often dormant than not. Early on, a programme of chemo sent it into remission for nobody knew how long; perhaps months, perhaps more. The mystery span of time turned out to be a full five years, during which the doctors worked with some success on subsidiary problems in my chest and my immune system, and I was able to function professionally almost as well as President Bartlet in *The West Wing*, whose undeclared disease did not inhibit him in his capacity to bomb the Middle East, outfox Chinese diplomats, or deal with the frightening facial mobility of Stockard Channing in a fit of anger. But not long ago my main event came back, to be faced by a medical opponent that might not have existed had it been smart enough to come back earlier. Now it is being held in check by a powerful new chemo drug called Ibrutinib. The drug's muscular name ("I, Brutinib. You, Olanzapine") sounds like the hero of one of those post-*Conan* movies starring some stack of sculpted tofu who will never be Arnold Schwarzenegger. But you won't find me disrespecting the package when the contents have such an impact. Saved from the unnerving blood-count plunge which set in when my lurking ailment came out of remission, I'm back to having time to burn. Though I haven't really got a chance, I haven't got an end date either. I'm not off the hook, but the hook is holding me upright; and it doesn't even hurt, which makes me a lot luckier than some of the people I see at the hospital.

In the five years before the latest crisis, I used up a lot of my blessed supply of extra time by reading. When Yale kindly asked me to write a little book about what I had been reading lately, I could barely fit what I had to say into the space allowed. There were always more books getting into my house, and readers of *Latest Readings* might easily have got the idea that reading books was all that I was doing with my enforced leisure. But I was also viewing, and I mean viewing everything. You might ask how a man who spent his days with the major poems of Browning could wish to spend his evenings with the minor movies of

Chow Yun-fat, but I could only reply that it was a duplex need buried deep in my neural network. Even in my weakness, my age-old, oil-burning TV and DVD habit (which had once been a VHS habit, but the dealers re-upped with some great new stuff) had not grown less. But the advent of the critically credentialed TV epic, niftily slotted into a folding sleeve, amplified a long-term addiction into a form of brain-scrambling suicide, because I wasn't just watching the new and often wonderful box sets, I was also continuing to watch, on the sludge channels, multiple rescreenings of the kind of old and not at all wonderful James Bond movie in which Roger Moore wears a flared safari suit and emits quips in close-up that achieve the difficult feat of making you remember Sean Connery's similar epigrams as rivaling the table talk of Oscar Wilde. For honesty's sake, if I was going to give an account of how I dealt with the new, high-end product, I would have to place my response in the context of the established brain patterns of someone who still felt compelled to switch on yet another screening of *Salt* and wait to see whether Angelina, when jumping from truck to truck through a blizzard of gunfire, might this time miss her mobile aiming-point and smack the speeding concrete highway with her improbably lush lips.

Once again I had more to say, going in, than the book could possibly hold. What to call it? *Latest Viewings* sounded too self-referential. My younger daughter Lucinda, whose key role in this enterprise will emerge in the telling, wanted me to call it *Band of Thrones*, thereby conflating the titles of the two box sets that could be thought of as bookends for our total viewing experience stretched over several years. Yes, we were in it together, initially in fair moderation with *The Sopranos* and *The West Wing*, and then, when the true, raging binge passion had set in, from our second viewing of *Band of Brothers* all the way through to the fifth season of *Game of Thrones*. We jumped together on the night before D-Day and we defended the Wall together against armies of tediously repellent CGI White Walker zombies. Indeed we had been in it together—the entire family had—since *The Sopranos* and *The West Wing* had introduced us all to the dizzy new pleasure of watching more than one episode of the same show in a single evening.

But surely three episodes was the maximum possible. Serious people had to retire for the night. It was Lucinda and I who pushed it all the way to four and even five; and now, every Saturday in the tiny parlor of my house of books, we binge-watch at that heady rate. Together, we may well be the only people in the world who have ever watched five episodes of *The Following* in succession without succumbing to catatonia. Would Kevin Bacon ever meet a character who was not a serial killer? That question kept us awake instead of putting us to sleep. How you can do that much watching without using up the universe is a question we will get to later. For now, enough to say that *From the Bada Bing to King's Landing* seemed like a possible title: a bit *entre nous*, perhaps, a bit *dans*, but it could be supplemented by an academically respectable subtitle: *A Study in the Imperialistic Accumulation of Mythical Milieux*. After all, this is a serious cultural subject.

Well no, perhaps it isn't, but it's still vital: the new mythology gets into everything, and the first thing it gets into is the old mythology. At my writing desk, after a lifetime of failing to engage with Spenser's *The Fairie Queene*, I at last engaged with it, and it struck me that the fair Duessa, the shape-changing femme fatale who causes so much trouble for the Red Cross Knight, has affinities with Melisandre, the scarlet woman in *Game of Thrones* who causes so much trouble for Stannis Baratheon among others. But when you think about it, this is a strange thought to be struck with.

It's as if classic literature had faded into the mind's background, and images encountered on the screen had become one's first frame of cultural reference. In view of this possibility, it becomes a positive likelihood that for the next generation they will be the *only* frame of reference. It's a new, pervasive, and irresistible vocabulary of the imagination. Familiar with it, one gets caught up in conversations in which properties of screen stories have the common currency once held by stories from the page. In Renaissance times the bright young people knew what they were talking about when they made glancing references to Ovid's *Metamorphoses*. Now the bright young people, although they are perhaps already turning into the bright early-middle-aged people, know what they are talking about when they say that two of their friends are like Josh Lyman and Donna Moss, or that another friend is a Zoe Barnes in the making, and could end up getting pushed under a train.

Even in the relative isolation imposed on me by my bad health, I have been unable to help noticing that any watercooler conversation about the screen stories tends to be at least as learned, allusive, and interesting as any critical analysis on the page. And as the television age has developed all over the world, so this critical language has increased its scope, providing a far more successful lingua franca than was ever the case with Esperanto. Only about a million of the earth's human inhabitants at any given time can read a page of anything in Esperanto. Yet we learn from the novels of Ahdaf Soueif that just before Egypt went to war with Israel in 1973, the smart set in Cairo were watching ancient reruns of *Peyton Place* on TV. When I was filming in India in 1995, the Bombay movers and shakers were all referring to the latest episodes of *The Bold and the Beautiful*, and they presumed that I shared their familiarity with that show's intricacies. In fact, I hadn't seen anything of that show in several years, but even as I dredged my memory, I was reaching the conclusion, surely correct, that the secret of American cultural imperialism's success lay exactly in this globally recognizable frame of reference, a cultural paste that spread straight from the fridge, like soft butter. Once it had penetrated behind the iron curtain, the viewers didn't have to understand the economics of capitalism to gauge the emblematic significance of Sue Ellen Ewing in *Dallas*. All they had to do was take a look at the gleam of her lip gloss as it wobbled in space while she worked her trick of mouthing a silent secondary line of dialogue to accompany the first. All they had to see was J.R.'s car, or even just his hat.

Not to mention his teeth: as the marvelous Croatian journalist Slavenka Drakulić tells us in her book *Café Europa*, Western teeth on their own would have been enough to bring down the Wall. Western TV never needed to spell a message out: it was all message, and still is. (When those irascible imams and mullahs said we just want your TV sets, we don't want your programmes, they meant we don't want *any* of your programmes, because there are none of them that might not feature a woman driving a car unpunished, or having her hand shaken by a man.) By now, the language in which we discuss Western TV penetrates the image all the way to the wallpaper. This book, I can already tell, will be written in just such an allusive language. I don't mean that serious students of this new Golden Age of Television (I place the capital letters to flag my suspicion that our acceptance of the term might need to be questioned once the euphoria dies down) are wasting their time. Indeed they have made vital contributions already. Brett Martin's book *Difficult Men*, which gives us the background to the big shows and the big show-runners (a handy term for the person in charge, especially when she is a woman), is a good shot at outlining the historical frame-work of the box set movement, even if, with its emphasis on the cable output, it pays too little attention to Aaron Sorkin's network breakthrough with *The West Wing*. And out there in Australia, my compatriot James McNamara, by so ably analyzing the wave of American achievement in his long article "The Golden Age of Television?" has already made a global contribution to cultural analysis. All he needs to do now is to reframe the article as a book, add-ing a couple of chapters to show why the Australian shows *Underbelly* (a scare fest about criminals) and *Rake* (a laugh riot about lawyers) ought to be in the canon. The reason is simple: they're gripping, and that always has to be the first consideration. Without that, complication and sophistica-tion count for nothing, or else you'd actually be enjoying the later novels of Henry James.

There will always be formal scholarly work to be done. But it will be done best if contact is not lost with the tone of common speech in which habitual consumers discuss the product; a tone not all that far from the voluble conge-niality with which they pass the popcorn. Binge-watching is a night out, even when you spend the whole day in. It's a way of being. (As Sartre unaccountably failed to note in his book *Being and Nothingness*, "binge" and "being" are anagrams of each other.) We begin to esteem this way of being at its true worth when we realize that the creators of the brain food that we are wolfing down are at least as involved in it, at the level of imagination, as we are ourselves. From Homer until now, and onward to wherever the creaking fleet of *Battlestar Galactica* will go in the future, there never was, and never will be, a successful entertainment fueled by pure cynicism. Even the people who once made the final, foundering episodes of *The Love Boat* had to reach into the depths of their well of feeling. They just didn't have to reach very far. And when we, alive now in this amazing era of creativity, click on Play All and settle back to watch every season of *The Wire* all over again, we should try to find a moment, in the midst of such complete absorption, to reflect that the imagined world being revealed to us for our delight really is an astounding and yet necessary achievement, even though we will always feel that we need an excuse for doing nothing else except watch it. We are well occupied. We are taking a long view.

Taking that long view, we should soon realize that we have been saved. The rack of box sets has provided the antidote for two kinds of disappointment. The long-form

TV series gives us reason to take heart when we see the commitment to dramatic fiction of the terrestrial broadcasters shriveling under the pressure of competition from the semicreative phenomenon which has somehow managed to bless itself with the misleading name of reality television. To use the term "semicreative" is, in most cases, putting it a bit high, but it has to be admitted that a reality format takes quite a lot of thinking up.

Sometimes the thinking is inspired, and a British show like *Big Brother* or *I'm a Celebrity Get Me Out of Here* comes lurching and belching into existence, dauntingly well equipped to leave a great broadcasting system looking crippled by its own gentility. At other times, all you get is something like the British show *Jump*, in which minor celebrities were equipped with skis and goaded into jumping off the end of a very short ramp, to the astonishment of nobody who was watching, and very soon nobody was. Either way, hit or miss, the period of creativity lasts only as far as the moment when the format is held to be established. After that, nothing happens on the mental level except accountancy. The great appeal of such stuff to the more soulless brand of television executive—not necessarily brainless, but always morally obtuse—is that it costs

next to nothing. The disadvantage is that intelligent viewers would rather watch almost anything else. In Britain,
the main channels still come up with the occasional stretch
of must-see fiction like *Downton Abbey* (i.e. the kind of period piece that the Americans are flatteringly pleased to im-
port under the general title of Masterpiece Theatre), and
there is always yet another show about a gifted but rebel-
lious middle-ranking policeman banished to a provincial
seaside town who redeems his reputation by solving the
sort of murder case in which everyone in the district is a
suspect. (When an actor famous for playing Dr. Who was
cast as the middle-ranking policeman, he grew a weird
half-beard to prove that he was serious, thereby becoming,
I thought, the only weirdly half-bearded middle-ranking
policeman in England. I thought he looked like D. H. Lawrence after an unsuccessful night with Frieda, but one of
my female advisers assures me that I am underestimating
both the prevalence and the attractiveness of the weird
half-beard.) Now that Inspector Morse is dead, there is always a show centered on the young Morse, or on his assistant Lewis, or on the young Lewis, or on Lewis's assistant
Hathaway. (One day there will be a show about Hathaway's
assistant when young.) The carved limestone Oxford set-

tings look delectable, but in time they can make you long to watch David Caruso standing sideways against the glittering vista in *CSI Miami* and taking off his dark glasses before putting them on again: not normally something that an intelligent viewer longs for.

But regular viewers can be excused for finding that the pickings have grown thin. If they go out to the movies, however, they meet the second kind of disappointment, because most of the new movies are blockbusters scaled up from Marvel comics or video games: source material in which young people are reputedly interested. Older people usually aren't, so back they limp to the television set, having invested in some form of software that gives them multiple channels. Superficially this looks like the answer. Even the cheapest package will have half a dozen channels full of everything in the *CSI* franchise, whether set in Las Vegas, Miami, or New York. (There is a capital joke in *Entourage* when the hopeless actor Johnny Drama talks of getting a part in *CSI Minneapolis*.) There are infinite supplies of *Law and Order*. They also run movies all the time, and some of the movies, even though made quite recently, are of the old type in which, if the white hats fought the black hats, the mayhem was confined within the limit of physical likelihood. But increasingly all the movies that screen on the sludge channels look as if they were designed to be there. When battle is joined, martial arts are employed. And they are not just the routinely astonishing martial arts of the *Kung Fu* and Bruce Lee type. They are magic martial arts. Actors, usually devoid of other characteristics, have the ability to rise twisting into the air and somersault over the heads of their opponents. You will see even big-name actors such as Keanu Reeves doing this. Once I had seen him doing it a few times, I never wanted to see him doing anything. And Keanu in the *Matrix* movies is at the top of the list of somersaulting heroes, along with Hugh Jackman in the *X-Men* movies. Milla Jovovich, the most beautiful face in creation, is reduced to the status of a cartoon as she somersaults through a cavalcade of robotized assailants: she wields a blade that shatters them like glass. Two blades. And a gun.

What eyes, but what idiocy. Further down the list, with less of the aerial maneuvering but even more reliance on the mad delusion that feet and bare hands can defy weapons, you get Jean-Claude Van Damme. Determined students are often ready to insist that a cliché meathead hero is sometimes in a good movie, and in Jean-Claude's case this is sometimes almost true: *Timecop* isn't bad. And even Jason Statham, whose usual fate is to spend half the movie employing his kick-boxing skills to wipe out one of those circular, inward-facing clusters of heavies who kindly make the mistake of throwing their guns away and attacking him one at a time, is possibly the right guy to star in *The Bank Job*, where you can just about imagine how his effortful cockney accent might charm the expensive pants off Saffron Burrows. Steven Seagal, his brow creased with the effort of wondering how he came to put on weight despite his diet of Asian health food, can still frighten a whole platoon of the Yakuza by the way he moves toward them with confident slowness, slowly advancing one pudgy hand in front of the other. But by the time you get down to Vin Diesel, you have to be the kind of viewer who gets an automatic reflex thrill out of watching a muscleman in a vest doing nothing except somersault to evade bullets, kick people in the head, and drive a car. You have to be a zombie: although let's not even get into the topic of zombies and vampires, who not only populate the big screen in the majority of all movies made for it but also populate those movies that never get as far as the big screen, and instead invade the small one with shambling armies of the undead and chorus lines of otherwise pretty actors of both main genders made portentous with heavy eye makeup, thus to convey the strain of combining procreative passion with a thirst for blood. If only Buffy could have slain them all.

People who worry about the effect of all this junk on the next generation probably aren't worried enough about themselves. From where I'm sitting, screen trash becomes an extinction event. See enough somersaulting actors and you'll have the sort of dreams that make you fall out of bed. In recent years, during this thematic collapse and ethical putrefaction of the film industry, there would have been little to save us from cortical decay if not for the providential rise of the box set. If you ever doubt the value of watching the buildup to a mealtime massacre in *Game of Thrones*, think of that sequence in *The Return of the King* that has Orlando Bloom bringing down the Mumakil, one of those mythical horned beasts which have been eating up the blue-screen sequences ever since *The Empire Strikes Back*. Orlando's victory over a digital effect took bundles of money and a factory full of the kind of IT expertise that can morph a film star into a digital double of himself, but the Red Wedding wipeout of a bunch of real live actors in the ninth episode of the third season of *Game of Thrones* took thought. The essential difference between a good box set drama and a comic-book movie's relentless catalogue of mechanized happenings is that the first thing leaves you with something to discuss, and the discussion becomes part of the experience. The second thing does all your reacting for you. The recent remake of *Total Recall* has immeasurably more advanced special effects than the original, but on the human level it doesn't even have Arnie. When a movie is nothing but spectacle, it is asking us to switch off our brains: a baleful modern precept of which Leni Riefenstahl was merely the pioneer. The will triumphs.

Nevertheless, the new Golden Age of Television, supposing that it exists, can't possibly leave Hollywood behind, and not just because Los Angeles is where most of its products come from. The show-runners and the writers, even at their most original, are drawing on a heritage. Just as, in Hollywood, there has always been an actor called Harrison Ford, so there have always been codes of allowable behavior. There was a time when screen lovers, even if they were supposed to be married, could not lie on the same bed unless the man had one foot on the floor. One of the reasons why the box set screenwriters are so determined to populate the screen with a writhing orgy is their accurate perception that liberty is being furthered: what they do now depends on their knowledge of what once could not be done. In fact, they know that kind of thing about movies and the media better than they know the world. (It might be a case of critical wish fulfillment to suppose that Martin Scorsese got his knowledge of mean-streets violence from spending his childhood with the bad boys: it's much more likely that his strict mother told him to stay away from them, and that he got most of his frame of reference from books and the movies.) The creative teams of today are not really abandoning the idea of codes of acceptability; but they do modify them, and in the box sets they are usually modifying them toward a humane and thoughtful maturity, thereby releasing the intelligent appreciation of the facts of life that generations of creative people were previously compelled to disguise. (*Californication* is essentially a sex fantasy from the mind of Cecil B. DeMille that arrives on screen without having to go by way of Babylon or ancient Rome.) The actors now may curse much more on screen, but they are even less likely than they once were to say anything provocative to those professing to be outraged by transgressions in the direction of sexism, racism, or any other patrol areas of political

correctness. In fact one of the inherent conflicts within recent television is the tension between the urge to speak
freely and the convention by which politically incorrect
vocabulary must be avoided. You could write a whole the-
sis about how modern ideological sensitivities rewrite the
past. It goes without saying that you must tread carefully
if you want to republish *The Nigger of the Narcissus* under
its original title, even though a great writer wrote it. But
now that anybody who once might have been called black
has to be called an African American (unless, like Idris Elba
in *The Wire*, he was born in Hackney and raised in East
Ham), it becomes problematic to refer, without trigger
warnings, to an innocent old movie that happened to have
the word "black" in its title. I thought for a while of writing a treatise about the politically inspired linguistic cleans-
ing of the past and calling it *The Beige Shield of Falworth*.

But then I thought again, and decided to write this book
instead. Soon the process of historical oblivion that Peter
Bogdanovich was the first to warn us about—the process
by which, if you tell young people about Charlton Heston's performance as Moses, they not only haven't heard
of Moses, they haven't heard of Charlton Heston—will
extend to embrace Tony Curtis, a man whose fame, which

reached to the whole world in my youth, had already waned by the time I interviewed him. Perhaps time, if left un-opposed, will always Sanforize itself into some form of in-telligible fiction, which we discuss with one another all the more learnedly because we don't really understand what Putin is up to in Ukraine, or what, whatever it is, can be done about it. The names of the buttons we push in order to make this new heritage roll before our eyes are under-stood by everyone. We all know how to make the sane per-son's decision to watch the episodes one at a time or the bingewatcher's decision to play every episode on the disc. And there's my title: *Play All*. There was a time when that instruction didn't even exist. But now it's in our lives, and especially it's in the lives of those of us who have run so short of time that time no longer matters, and who are thus able to choose exactly what we want to see next. Shall I spend the better part of tomorrow afternoon making fur-ther inroads into the novels of Sir Walter Scott? Or shall I join my daughter in watching four episodes of *Dexter?* All right, five. Followed by a learned discussion of whether *The Following* might not have been a bit more plausible if Kevin Bacon's character, instead of merely chasing serial killers, had serially killed them.

The Ducks Have Left the Pond

A HUGE MAN is on the pool patio outside his house in New Jersey. In the close-up, Tony Soprano's face is creased with effort on its various levels and terraces. He is wondering where the ducks have gone. Is he reflecting that they must have left for the winter, or has it occurred to him that he, too, might be subject to divine will? *Why hast Thou forsaken me?* It helps that the face belongs to James Gandolfini. It is massive. Even at only a first visit to the show, the viewer will already have realized that Gandolfini, who can so easily fade into the background in his movies, looms immensely on television. From *Get Shorty* you can barely remember him: he was just a failed torpedo that John Travolta threw downstairs. But in *The Sopranos* he is a magnetic mountain, pulling toward him all legends of haunted loneliness and seismic inner violence. Charles Laughton looked that size in *The Hunchback of Notre Dame.* In *I,*

Claudius, Brian Blessed as Augustus, his cheeks puffed with makeup, is eaten alive by his old-age worries about whether his family is up to inheriting the empire whose dizzy limits were set by him in the sly power of his vigor. Gatsby wondered what the green light was worth if it could not give him Daisy. Holden Caulfield wondered what happened to the ducks when the pond froze over. You don't have to contemplate Tony's hulking yet tormented image for long before realizing how futile it is to trace the show to its origins, as if the fact that its basic narrative device is a straight lift from the movie *Analyze This* were somehow proof that *The Sopranos* is not *sui generis*.

Of *course* it isn't. It's got everything in it, including all the *Godfather* movies except the bad scenes in *Godfather III* when the plot goes so haywire you get time to wonder about Al Pacino's hairpiece. Characters in *The Sopranos* can play all the characters in *The Godfather* movies. Loafing at the Bada Bing or outside Satriale's Pork Store, they quote *Godfather* dialogue by the yard. They can do that without crashing the vehicle because they're in a bigger story than the one they're quoting. Anyone who sat through the action-free story line of *Rubicon* will testify that when the leading characters started referring to *Three Days of the*

Condor, the show was doomed, because the viewer could not recover from the enforced reminder that the show wasn't a patch on the movie. It was three hours of the condor at the very most. *The Sopranos* is at least three *Godfather* movies plus *The Magnificent Ambersons* and Abel Gance's *Napoleon*. Not that it has all that much sheer spectacle. But it does have inner scope.

The Sopranos is so capacious that it can sabotage itself and still keep your devotion. Tony's liability of a sister Janice, as played by Aida Turturro, is such a flake that she made some viewers switch off. Those many millions of us who stayed loyal weren't just fascinated by the post-hippie fecklessness of Janice's disaster-strewn curriculum vitae— I especially appreciated that she was still drawing insurance checks for carpal tunnel syndrome acquired from her not very strenuous period of actuating a coffee machine— we were fascinated by the effect she had on Tony. She enraged him, and usually when people enrage Tony he gets rid of them. They end up bumped off, cut up, and sunk in the landfill. But he can't do that to members of his immediate family. There is no real limit to his power, but there is a limit to his ruthlessness. In this respect, he's a bit like us: or so we would like to think. (We would like to think that our omnipotence is reined in by moral scruple.) In the Brian de Palma movie *Scarface*, Tony Montana (Al Pacino) doesn't hesitate to ruin his sister's happiness. Tony Soprano does hesitate, even when we, his audience, are mentally egging him on, aching for the moment when he switches his huge capacity for violence to the necessary task of eliminating this pain in his butt, but also sadly aware that he will once again talk himself into accommodating her crazy needs. So there she stays, making our hearts sink from week to week. And we stay too: eloquent testimony to the show's psychological grip.

Tony's nephew and possible heir apparent Christopher is potentially an even bigger liability to Tony's premiership, and therefore to the show's narrative spine, than his batso sister. Christopher is played by Michael Imperioli, an actor with talent to spare—some of the spare talent, later on in the show's evolution, was brilliantly employed in episodes he not only acted in but wrote and directed—so he won't mind having it said that the basic equipment of his facial appearance tilts him toward the kind of role in which you wouldn't give him a mad dog's chance of remaining stable. Right from his first fits of anger in the opening episodes, and more and more every time he promises to straighten out, Christopher demonstrates that his hair-trigger impulsiveness is incurable: he will never get it under control. It isn't a help that he lives in preconnubial bliss with the beautiful Adriana, whose only gift is for wondering why a fluttering of her eyelashes is not in itself sufficient to vacuum the carpets; but Christopher needs no help from her or anyone to turn any project into a screw-up. Even when he shifts his ambitions from crime to the arts, his instinct, when he encounters an obstacle in the music business—and the main obstacle, of course, is that he is without talent—is to run off and snort a hillock of cocaine, or pull a gun, or both. Most of what we know about Christopher, Tony knows too, sooner or later. And sooner or later Tony should have sidelined him. In *Goodfellas* Imperioli played a minor character who irritated Joe Pesci and therefore got shot in the foot: proof of the Pesci character's uncontrollable impatience and unreliability. In *The Sopranos*, Christopher has those characteristics, and we would have been quite content if Tony had dealt with him by confining his role to sorting garbage, or just by killing the fool. But several seasons go by before Tony can face that Christopher might be a problem with only one solution. This time lapse would matter less if Tony were just exercising his usual reluctance to wreak destruction on his own blood-line. But there is a bigger consideration: Tony is also meant to be the man in charge of an organization, not just a criminal but a master criminal. Why, then, is he even contemplating giving the succession to a psychopath? Why can't this king among wise guys be more wise?

Merely to ask the question is a sign of how expectations have been sentimentalized by the movies, and of how the box set, with more time to explore psychology, has done something to save us from the kind of uplift that lowers the IQ. Perhaps taking a tip from *I, Claudius,* which the show-runner David Chase saw when he was growing up, Chase makes Tony, his modern Augustus, cunning but not all-knowing. Especially Tony is not wise about the interior workings of those closest to him: a failing not uncommon among clever people. In the movies, when a central figure is set up to be smart, there is usually not enough time to show him being dumb. Tony Montana in *Scarface* is a rare instance, in the movies, of a far-seeing crime overlord who also behaves like a dolt, and even then we are encouraged to believe that he might never have put a foot wrong if the white powder had not eaten his brains. A much more typical movie big shot is the Godfather himself, Don Vito

Corleone. As played in his youth by Robert De Niro, Don Corleone is smarter than anybody else. As played in his maturity and old age by Marlon Brando, Don Corleone is still smarter than anybody else, and in addition has picked up the habit of expressing his wisdom in epigrams, like Seneca or Marcus Aurelius. All over the world as you read these words, there are mediocrities sitting in midlevel offices muttering, "Keep your friends close, keep your enemies closer." (Actually we never see the old man saying that: but his youngest son Michael, another natural guru, remembers that he said it.) To hear the Don talking, one would think that the script's basic assumption that the mob functions as an effective substitute for America's defective system of justice might have something to it. After all, who, except the unjustly powerful, gets hurt by Don Corleone's family, ruled as it is by his all-comprehending benevolence? And to whom else can the little guy turn, if not to the Godfather? In reality, there can only be a single answer to both questions: almost everybody gets hurt, and especially the little guy.

As John Dickie demonstrates in his excellent book *Cosa Nostra*, the Sicilian hoodlums, on their home island, were never dedicated to protecting the little guy against his getting soaked by the rich landlords; they were dedicated to joining the rich landlords in soaking the little guy even further. Considered from the viewpoint of social analysis, the great merit of *The Sopranos*, vis-à-vis the *Godfather* trilogy, is that it accepts this fact and shows how it works in the modern age. On the level of raw violence, the street gardener who has signed the wrong contract simply has his limbs broken until he signs the right one. If he ran out of limbs he would have his head broken: but it isn't necessary, because he has already signed, or at any rate made the strangled noise that a hospitalized man in traction makes in lieu of a written agreement. Though outright mayhem happens rarely in the show—it doesn't have to, because the mere threat is usually enough—when it does happen it usefully reminds you that a character like Pauley Walnuts, for all the linguistic charm by which he evokes his aging upper arms ("as wrinkled as an old lady's cunt"), is essentially someone who will bend an innocent civilian to his will by beating him to jelly. On the more subtle level of mental torture, Artie the restaurateur, who by his gift for foolish investments has brought his enterprise to bankruptcy, is saved by a loan from Tony. Being saved by Tony ensures that he will be enslaved forever. Artie is a family friend but he is not family, so friendship earns him nothing except misery: he will have to keep smiling while he continues to let Tony eat for free. Once, Tony and his family ran up a tab that was only rarely paid. Now it will never be paid. Artie's torment shows in his compulsorily merry face, and shows the true cost of being in the mob's grip.

This is a petty but essentially true level of reality that is nearly absent in the realm of Don Corleone, where the norms of behavior are set by his presidential forbearance. Protection rackets are barely mentioned. The Don won't allow the family to go into the drugs business. He has an answer to anyone who objects: the true business of a crime family is to deal with natural human weaknesses, such as the need for women. Drugs are too dirty. The Don's favorite son Santino, known to all as Sonny, quite likes the idea of moving into drugs, but Sonny—very believably played by James Caan as a sexual athlete with a muscle between his legs and another muscle between his ears—is impulsive and lacks a moral sense, and eventually pays for those failings with his life, inspiring his father not only to paternal tears but also to the silliest line in the trilogy, the line about how Tattaglia "could never have outfought Santino." Since all the evidence of the script up to that point has indicated that Santino was so impulsive that anybody in America including his own mother could have outfought him with ease, we must conclude either that the Don is not so smart after all or that some of the epic story's themes are not in touch with one another. The second conclusion seems the more persuasive. The governing notions that there can be an ethical crime empire and that it can be ruled by an all-wise wise guy refuse to add up either separately or together.

The Sopranos, less prone to filtering out the poison from the atmosphere that all must breathe in an ambience of potential but omnipresent violence, digs deeper into character, pushing on beyond the cartoon outline and probing the soul. In the *Godfather* trilogy, the mother figure is the revered presence who can't be asked to face the prospect of Fredo's death until she herself dies. After she goes, Fredo finally goes too, in that sad and beautiful movie moment out on the lake. But in *The Sopranos*, which is less like a movie, an ugly truth outranks a pretty image; and the mother figure is Livia, who is all evil. Quite possibly her name is a direct acknowledgment by David Chase of his debt to *I,*

Claudius, in which the wife of Augustus, as played by Siân Phillips, is an elegant wit. The mother of Tony Soprano is a style-free scold. She is such a drain on the spirit that it takes us almost as long as Tony to figure out that she might want him dead, although we get a powerful hint of her wishes when she helps Uncle Junior (Dominic Chianese) to get the idea that a world without Tony might have its advantages. While taking note of the large area of psychology which is opened up by the mere possibility that Tony has a killer of a mother, we should step aside at this point and note also that the long exploration and development of such a character is something that only the long-form TV series has ever done; that no movie could ever do; and that it presents an actor, or in this case an actress, with the opportunity of a lifetime. In her previous career, Nancy Marchand was the go-to patrician performer for any role requiring poise, breeding, and distinction. Just by her screen presence she put you in mind of Kay Graham, Jackie Kennedy, and Queen Elizabeth II. In the TV series *Lou Grant* she was the newspaper proprietress who ruled Ed Asner with a scepter of crystal. In the movie remake of *Sabrina* she was the matriarch whose well-run realm made it plausible that the chauffeur's daughter might once have

sat dreaming in a tree, outside the family circle and looking in. Along with her distinguished early career on Broad-
way, all this history of polish and dignity came with her
into *The Sopranos*, where she was asked to trash it for years
on end. She rubbished herself triumphantly, keeping her
stature but setting a torch to her personal charm. She ended
up even scarier than Janice: something you would hesitate
to say about Madame Mao.

This deliberate misuse, or new use, of our expectations
about an actor is one of the features a long-form story can
offer, because there is time to justify it, making us not so
much think again as think more deeply. But here again,
one shouldn't grow starry eyed about the opportunity offered to an older actor to consolidate a career. A younger
actor might feel stifled, and try to run. Rob Lowe probably
saw himself in a trap when he played Sam Seaborn in *The
West Wing*, and took the opportunity to become the headline act in *The Lyon's Den*. He might not necessarily have
been making the same mistake as David Caruso made when
he left *NYPD Blue*. The switch might have worked out.
The TV show that makes you famous doesn't necessarily
close out the future. Edie Falco was Tony Soprano's wife
Carmella right until the show's last moment, and she went

on to be the headliner in *Nurse Jackie,* where her background as the woman who dared to steal some of Tony's
money might even have helped her convince us as the
nurse who combined a drug habit with her duties of care.
In general, however, it must be said that a long role in a big
show is hard to survive. James Gandolfini, after ceasing to
be Tony, went onward to many projects as an actor and
producer, but there is anecdotal evidence that he never
really emerged from prison, and that he died in there, still
troubled about the way the walls of fame—Tony's fame,
not his—closed in to crush him.

Once again, sentimental expectations threaten. One
mustn't suspect Gandolfini of being in mental turmoil just
because he looked like it. He was an actor, and one of the
essential components of Tony's character was for him to
seem always a little lost, even in the thrill of battle. (I think
often of the day when he takes his daughter Meadow to
view a school and leaves her for a while because he has
just spotted an unpunished snitch whom he must kill. He
doesn't look as if he wants to do it. He just has to.) As
played by De Niro and Brando, Don Corleone is all of a
piece: we aren't asked to imagine him in mental trouble:
indeed, he draws much of his resonance from the flattering

way he makes us feel that we ourselves, with all our mighty powers, might be in mental trouble for not being fully integrated like him, doing what he must and facing no psychic cost except sadness after one of his sons gets killed. As played by Al Pacino in *Godfather III*, however, Michael Corleone, the Don reborn, needs to talk to a priest, because he can't quell the nagging question of whether murdering his own brother was right or wrong. But in one of the longest movies ever to have been a mile too short, there is no room in the script to explore the doubt. In *The Sopranos*, there is a time scale to match the slow scope of the main character's war within himself. There are few big shoot-outs—the *Godfather* trilogy has a war in each movie—but there is room for Tony to do seriously what Paul Vitti (Robert De Niro again) in *Analyze This* does only on the level of comedy: open up to the shrink. Watching the show from season to season on TV, we spend years finding out that Tony has problems with his mother and father, just like us. Even when binge-watched, it's a very gradual unfolding. But it's a richly productive device, as even the psychiatrist Dr. Melfi becomes part of the wider examination of motives in the criminal panorama. Lorraine Bracco might not be funny like Billy Crystal, but she is fully human, and this fact turns out to be especially telling when she gets raped in a parking garage by some young lout so stupid that he lets her see his face. Later on, still traumatized, she happens to see that same face in a poster celebrating the Employee of the Month in a pizza house. She tells her fiancée that if she gave the name to Tony he would squash her attacker "like a bug." She doesn't. Those are the bare bones of a secondary plot.

But the psychological ramifications are manifold, and tend to put the viewer, and especially the male viewer, on the spot. We already know from previous episodes that Tony is attracted to Melfi. (Time has elapsed since the young Lorraine Bracco in *Someone to Watch Over Me,* one of the rare makeout movies ever aimed at adulterers, played a cop's wife so attractive that not even Mimi Rogers in distress could tempt him away for long; but she's still enchanting.) When betraying his wife, Tony's usual choice of collaborator is a prostitute or a lap-dancer, but he also has hankerings toward the up-market and educated, an inclination in keeping with his nervous admiration for brains and taste. (Tony has no inkling that his wife, Carmella, sharing exactly the same frustrated hunger, will fall in love with the imported button man Furio simply because of his fine European manners: Furio might bring her a carefully chosen packet of Italian biscuits for a nice surprise, whereas Tony would be more likely to give her a stolen car.) Tony is grudgingly able to accept Melfi's rejection of his advances, rationalizing her refusal of him as an assertion of her professional detachment. He finds it hard to believe, however, that she is not attracted to him: as a big, strong, and powerful man, he is used to the idea that any woman is attracted to him on some level. This assumption on his part seems arrogant until we realize that Melfi, if she does not find him attractive, does find his strength attractive. After the rape, her fiancée, a civilized civilian like you and me, can do nothing to help her except act as a listening post, and she can get a higher quality of listening from her own shrink, a multicameo role ably filled by Peter Bogdanovich. We are at liberty to guess—we are encouraged to—that she yearns for Tony's powers of protection and revenge. This reference to the power relationships that apply (let's say might apply) between the genders is a solvent for any fond beliefs we might harbor about desire having brains, and puts the substory in the same area as the rest of the show, which is the area of the jungle. No matter how refined she might have been in her current context, a woman propelled back to the original evolutionary environment is likely to look with favor on Tony if only to protect herself from all the other men who are like him but worse. You could even say that Lorraine Bracco has a right to find an alpha male. In *Someone to Watch Over Me* she almost lost one: the previously faithful cop husband played by Tom Berenger left her so that he could share high-tab percale sheets with the society princess who fell for him not solely because Berenger was, at the time, the most handsome actor in Hollywood, but because she was being hunted by a killer and needed a lover with some stopping power. That part of the story rang true. The romanticism was when he went home again. *The Sopranos* is notably free of the romantic impulse. Watching, we sometimes long for a romantic outcome, but we can give ourselves credit as re-alists for having chosen the wrong show to have watched.

Our tendency to take a romantic view comes from deep within us, and partly from a justifiable fear that the actual world is too raw to deal with. Whether art is better or worse for showing us the world's horrors unadorned is a tricky question, partly self-answered by the fact that it can't, beyond a certain point. If the screen were to show us the full horror of unrestrained violence, it would be impossible to watch. *The Sopranos* doesn't cosmeticize the emetic reality of mob rule, but it does soften it. When Big Pussy meets his end on Tony's boat, he is allowed his dignity. Ralphie, having asked to have his screaming voice silenced for seasons on end—the voice belongs to Joe Pantoliano, a ruthless expert at getting on your nerves—finally gets his, but while his ex-friends are cutting him up for disposal, he still provides us with one of the best *grand guignol* laughs in the show. Christopher, surprised, holds up Ralphie's head of hair, never having guessed that it was a wig. Tony knew; but we know that not even Tony knows everything. He doesn't know, and mustn't know, that Carmella loved Furio. The success of the show can be measured by the intensity with which we hope he won't find out; and yet we also can't suppress the knowledge that Carmella is at least half a willing collaborator in Tony's reign of terror, and that Furio, when out on a debt-collecting mission, is terror itself.

Even with this scope of psychological analysis, the show can't give you the whole truth: but at least the truth is not violated. Enough of the crime family's death dance of a way of life is evoked to make us worry about how it will be perpetuated: will Tony's son A.J. ever be up to inheriting the leadership, and what if his sister Meadow flourishes as an honest lawyer and goes on to bring the whole organization to where it belongs, in court if not in Guantanamo? Actually, we know what Meadow (Jamie-Lynn Sigler) goes on to do: she goes on to be Turtle's girlfriend in *Entourage*. But for the bingeing viewer that's a familiar analgesic effect; a nice reminder that the character, whether threatening or being threatened, is only acting. When *The Sopranos* is holding us in its unrivaled spell, however, we have to be anxious about whether Meadow's independence of mind— it's almost a government advertisement for the benefits of education—will bring her into deadly peril. If she has only her principles to hold at bay the weight of influence that Tony might eventually feel called upon to wield, she has little chance. She will need a gun, like the one that Janice goes to find when Vic, exercising the made man's traditional obligation when contradicted by a mere goomah, slaps her in the face. She shoots him dead. By our standards, he behaves better after that. But our standards aren't what drive the story; and that was the gate of discrepancy that the show opened when it started. When it finished, not even the ending satisfied our expectations. We expected a shoot-out, but life just went on, such as it was. The message was that our expectations had been too much shaped by what the screen had previously shown us, which was now changing.

Actors Airborne

THE NATURAL MODUS OPERANDI of the bingewatcher, having selected Play All in order to view a whole bunch of episodes on a disc, is to skip through the standard opening title sequence on each episode, especially when watching a show for the second or third time. But for at least two shows I have never done this, and have always watched the title sequence right through. One is *The Sopranos,* where the opening music—a piece of British rock and roll, oddly enough—is perpetually renewable in its pulse and color. The cutting from skyline to skyline of the drive through New Jersey seems part of the score, and you get to know its every bar so well that you know exactly where the twin towers should have been when they disappeared after the 9/11 disaster. The other is *Band of Brothers.* The opening sequence is so authoritative that Lucinda and I watch the whole thing every time. We are agreed that the way the stills and slo-mo clips are matched to the music couldn't be improved, and that the music is uncannily beautiful. Thus the range of tragic lyricism in which the young men, the airborne brothers in arms, will risk their lives together in combat, and some will die and some will not, is established at the start of each episode. For my generation, who were infants when our fathers left us behind at home and went away to fight, this pictured music, or musical picture, is intensely recognizable, as deeply serious as something so aesthetically satisfactory could be. But I was surprised to find that Lucinda felt the same. Her knowledge of World War II is all from books—Anthony Beevor's book *The Battle of Stalingrad* was her idea of a birthday present—but it is detailed and nuanced, and her standards of authenticity are high. It was from her reaction, not my own, that I reached a proper measure of the show's success in transmitting, without dilution or trivialization, the texture of the past into the future.

The boot-camp episode that opens the series is the basis of the show's monumental moral scope. Somewhere in the United States the members of Easy company are still safe from death, but they are at the mercy of their commanding officer, the madly authoritarian Lieutenant Herbert M.

Sobel, disturbingly played—against the comfortable expectations he brings from his role in *Friends*—by David
Schwimmer. Sobel is a Jew, so the first few episodes, during
which Easy company learns to march, run, and jump before being transferred to England and prepared for its
baptism of fire, are devoted to showing how the boys suf-
fer from the sadistic whims of the detestable Jewish guy
until they are saved by the unflinching integrity of the admirable WASP guy Sergeant (later Lieutenant, and finally
Major) Richard Winters, played by Damian Lewis, a British actor with a convincing American accent. (Like Dominic West, who plays in *The Wire*, Lewis was educated at
Eton, but the days are happily long gone when British actors couldn't throw their voices across the Atlantic: it's
not because so many of them are now more adaptable, it's
because so many of them are now more talented.) The
company's justified collective loathing for Sobel is put into
perspective as the show winds toward the last of its ten episodes, when the company stumbles on a concentration
camp and finds out at first hand what anti-Semitic preju-
dice has come to under the shield of Nazi power. Stephen
Spielberg, coproducer of the show along with Tom Hanks,
must be given credit for this range of treatment of a topic

close to his heart. It was Spielberg's movie *Schindler's List* that did most to get the look of the thing on screen within a decently respectful distance of what the original horrors must have been like. But *Schindler's List,* which is about how some were saved, has an element of wish fulfillment— Primo Levi would have said that the disaster was the story of those who were not saved—that *Band of Brothers* avoids.

In fact, *Band of Brothers* avoids nearly all the perennial Hollywood clichés, including those that linger even in its immediate progenitor *Saving Private Ryan,* the movie which set our current standards for a convincing battle scene. The story of how the last of Mrs. Ryan's sons gets brought back alive is a *Saturday Evening Post* story plus extras. Some of the extras are superb—try watching the climactic scenes in the village without becoming a fan of Edith Piaf—but the final effect is of a consolatory neatness. In *Band of Brothers* Hanks and his chief collaborator Erik Jendresen, with Spielberg signing off on the 120 million dollars of production costs (the show got back a quarter of a *billion* dollars from its DVD releases alone, but show business is a business: if you could be dead certain, going in, of getting a hit, everybody would be doing it), keep the consolation strictly limited, while increasing the range of incident into a whole new dimension. Take the *Private Ryan* care for texture and apply it over an area that compares for size like the Sistine ceiling to the Mona Lisa, and you've got the scope of *Band of Brothers*, which is big even when it is stuck in the back of a truck with the abrasive Bill Guarnere (Frank John Hughes) finally accepting that Winters might be a good fighting leader after all. It is big even when Malarkey (Scott Grimes), having returned to England after the carnage of the first drop in Normandy, picks up the laundry parcels for the boys who won't be coming back. It is big even when the exhausted medic Eugene Roe (Shane Taylor) gets back to the bombed ruins of Bastogne, looks for the nurse (Lucie Jeanne) whose merciful example he and we have come to depend on, and finds her gone. Her mere absence, registered in a few shots, has as much impact as the grand total of all the long battle scenes set in the Hürtgen forest.

By these means *Band of Brothers* helped to establish a ground rule for the long-form TV serial: that the range of emotional effect trumps spectacle. The night sequence where the planes arrive over Normandy and are chewed up by the flak, and some of the young men die even before they have gone into action, is hellishly well done: the CGI effects are almost up there with the authentic footage used in the Iwo Jima invasion sequence in *The Halls of Monte-zuma* all those decades ago. But the sequence in which the nurse simply fails to appear has an effect at least equal to it. And the effect is achieved by a lavishness that goes beyond an outpouring of budget; it is achieved by a lavishness of writing. Care has been taken. The true wealth of the box set always begins in the writer's room, where the cards that bear the names of the scenes and sequences are shifted around and further annotated until the episode reveals the nervous system from which it will expand into a living fiction: that is, into a manageable reality.

For convenience we can, and perhaps should, go on calling Spielberg and Hanks the auteurs of the show. But its writing, and its whole batch of directors, are enough to prove that the old idea of a single auteur setting the tone is as irrecoverably gone as the idea of a single-authored comedy show. That idea vanished long ago, when it was realized that Sid Caesar, more sketch comedian than stand-up, needed ideas from Mel Brooks, Neil Simon, Carl Reiner, Woody Allen and half a dozen others if he was to keep to his weekly schedule. The development of the big TV fiction series in recent times can be said to be measurable by the extent that drama adopted the working methods of comedy. The laughs were turned off but the communal effort was stepped up. Nevertheless, there are few writing teams without crucial figures, and Stephen Ambrose can be called a crucial figure in the gigantic effort that produced *Band of Brothers*. In all his books about the European War—*Citizens' Army* is particularly fine—he is keen to find an explanatory linear theme. For the theme of Easy Company's advance from its Georgia training camp to Berchtesgaden, the linear theme was given to him on a plate, but he deserves the principal initial credit for making the most of it. Ever since Hollywood started to put the classic myths and stories through the mincer to determine their essential elements, the select band who, guided by an all-wise commander, fight their way to the great prize had been a standard plotline. Go back as far as *A Walk in the Sun* and you still probably haven't gone back far enough, while if you go forward from there you will pass dozens of questing warrior bands before you eventually collapse with boredom among *The Wild Geese* and *Force Ten from Navarone*. Even *The Eagle Has Landed* is a quest movie: the boys aren't going to Berchtesgaden (Michael Caine, though playing a German officer, can't even *say* Berchtesgaden), but they are going in search of Churchill's scalp. You could even say that the formative ancestor of *Band of Brothers* was not *Saving Private Ryan* but that scuzzy old monster of a movie *The Dirty Dozen*, which was likewise made largely in England (at Borehamwood), gathered together an elite military force chosen from material as yet untouched by discipline (criminals, in fact), and sent it, under the command of Lee Marvin, in search of a radiant objective (a castle full of high-ranking German extras). (One further, but necessary, parenthesis: as a Marine on Saipan, Lee Marvin had two bullets put through him, an experience which made him a sour judge of Hollywood militaristic hokum. But an actor has to act.) In *Band of Brothers* the grail may be Göring's cache of fine wines, but the quest to reach it has every knightly virtue.

These virtues emanate from the characters: ordinary citizens temporarily in uniform, but up there like Arthur, Lancelot, and Galahad. It sounds simple, even hackneyed; but so do most of the classic plots (think of how often you have seen *The Terminator* under another title—even the heroine of a dud like *Hanna* might as well have been played by Arnie in a skirt), and structural analysis, like structuralism in general, is rarely informative about the only artistic

parameter that matters, which is quality. The simple outline of *Band of Brothers* is the framework for a lavish range
of nuance. The reason, while you are watching it, that you
spend no time being struck by the similarity to a thousand
plots is that you are continually being struck by subplots
that are subtle like nothing else you have ever seen. My
favorite example would be the way the preliminary scene
to the concentration camp revelation links up with what
comes next in a completely unpredictable yet entirely satisfactory way. Our intelligence officer, Captain Lewis Nixon
(engagingly played by Ron Livingston as a smart, witty
alcoholic), is caught by a German officer's widow (Suzanne
Roquette) trespassing in her house. Nixon accidentally
drops and breaks a framed photograph of her husband.
Nixon looks ashamed, as if conceding that her accusatory
stare is justified, and that he is indeed intruding, like a
looter. Later in the episode, after the concentration camp
is discovered, all the local Germans are brought to see it,
and to help shift and stack the emaciated bodies. Nixon,
watching them do this, sees the German officer's widow.
She catches him watching: her turn to look ashamed, but
of something much larger and more real. Whether the discrepancy between Nixon's transgression and Nazi Ger-

many's universal atrocity is dawning on her, or whether she will ever come to admit it, we just don't know: and as so often happens when it comes to subtlety, our not knowing is a mark of the authenticity. This linkage, the pathos, and the silent suggestion are all done with glances. A classic example of construction outranking dialogue, it can be fairly called a great piece of purely cinematic writing, and would not be less so if we could prove that the German officer's wife was borrowed from the Marlene Dietrich character in *Judgment at Nuremberg.* We can't ask screenwriters not to have seen movies: it's how they learn to write. We can only ask them not to forget historical reality, and to be loyal to the truth: it's how they learn to think.

A plenitude of such thoughtful effects makes *Band of Brothers* almost too successful to pick apart. To see why it is so subtly integrated, so resonant in its networks of suggestion—regard again the sharpness of the event when Sobel, near the end, *doesn't* salute Winters—you have to look at its unsuccessful sequel *The Pacific,* which is such a mess that all its components are sticking out so that you can see how they failed to join up. Perhaps Spielberg and Hanks were on a mission: they had wrapped up the war in Europe, now for the war in the Pacific. Speaking as someone whose family history was deeply affected by the war in the Pacific, I looked forward to what Spielberg and Hanks would do with the story, but it was evident from halfway into the first episode that they would not be able to do enough. The war in the Pacific had no holy grail that could be reached except in the form of the instrument of surrender that was eventually signed on the deck of the battleship *Missouri* in Tokyo bay. The war's main narrative line—the island-hopping campaign that brought the B-29s close enough to Japan so that they could stage the decisive bombing raids culminating in the use of the nuclear weapons—was inherently a story that progressed without ever taking shape, and this shapelessness is reflected all too well by the structure of the show, which is scattered over too many islands. Nevertheless, some order might have been imposed if a band of brothers could have been sent on a specific quest, even at the risk of echoing *The Naked and the Dead*. Norman Mailer confined his novel to the fictional island of Anopopei, and managed to cram a whole American social system into his frame. But the makers of *The Pacific* were true, too true, to the incoherence of their material. The leading characters, played by actors whom we tend not to remember because nobody who watched cared, are seldom in touch with one another, and there is no Nixon figure—a crucial omission, this—to give them the big picture. When they go on leave, it is to an Australia whose denizens are so prone to cliché that they might make an older viewer yearn for the comparative subtlety of the New Zealand pictured in the old movie *Battle Cry*, in which Van Heflin furrowed his brow and flexed his jaw in a military manner (he could do both those things at once) but at least the Kiwi girls had a few scraps of dialogue with which to set the Yank boys dreaming.

In *The Pacific* the Australian haven provides even fewer memorable scenes than the islands which the Yank boys invade in order to blast bunch after bunch of Japanese extras out of the jungle. Out they come running, spin around and fall down, as they have been doing ever since John Wayne pointed his prop gun at them in *The Sands of Iwo Jima*. Hour after hour, we seem to be watching the kind of old movie whose trite production values Spielberg was sent into the world to rescue us from. He did *The War of the Worlds* better than he did this. Even his epic comedy *1941* was better; and the only other thing that *1941* was better than was the nineteenth-century Irish potato famine. Even Clint Eastwood's two movies about Iwo Jima—a binational project that adds up to *Tora! Tora! Tora!* plus tunnels—look fresh when compared with the weary scenarios of *The Pacific*. All the amphtracks look real, but the troops who come splashing out of them have nothing real to say or do. At times the script sounds barely filmable, making you wonder how Hanks, of all people, could have okayed the project: the one thing any long-term star actor is sure to know is whether a script is ready for the cameras. The scripts of *The Pacific* were ready only for the bin. But the whole megabudget stretch of unleavened bread can tell you a lot about its successful predecessor: *The Pacific*, by what it doesn't have, is a testimony to what *Band of Brothers* has. The crucial ingredient is not realism of effect—a few hundred million dollars will buy you some of that— but a sense of complex reality. Watching *The Pacific* is like being shackled to the couch and forced to see *Pearl Harbor* for a second time. It almost makes you sorry that the Japanese lost. But there is no need to press the point, because *The Pacific* was forgotten instantly. It might have been forgotten even had it been better done. The series *Over There* was brilliantly conceived and should have made more impact than it did, but it was hampered by the distancing effect a war story tends to have when the enemy is nothing like us. The Arab opponents might as well have been Transformers. *The Pacific* had the same problem. In *Band of Brothers*, the opponent is us gone wrong, and we ourselves are at our best.

Sorkin on the Racing Line

BOTH *THE SOPRANOS* and *Band of Brothers* were HBO cable productions, and their collective impact might tend to persuade us that network television was left nowhere. But it's a law of the arts that a stylistic innovation gets instantly everywhere, like heat or cold; and in fact, even while HBO was still thinking of *Band of Brothers,* it was a network, NBC, that took the new long-look format in an unexpected new direction, with *The West Wing,* created by Aaron Sorkin. The word "created" always looks excessive when it pops up among the titles on a screen, but in Sorkin's case it fits. Working on his own, he could seldom do structure like an HBO team: he has a frat-house penchant for slapstick, and his idea of a climax can be a plaster ceiling falling on the hero's head. But *The West Wing* had so much growth potential that there was very soon no question of his working alone. Though he did much of the writing (possibly too much for his health) there was a whole organization toiling to keep him on the racing line—I often lapse into motor sport terminology when thinking about his work, because his mind is so quick—and he was left free to exploit his best gift, which is for the most elaborately eloquent dialogue since the great days of Hollywood screwball comedy in the late 1930s and early 1940s. Postwar mental torpor tried to kill all that glittering rapidity, but Sorkin brought it back to its full glory, having realized that an extended television serial format would give it more room to hurtle. He would have liked to work that act of resurrection for the movies, and he tried: the pages of dialogue that he was forced to leave out of his script for *The American President* were what gave him his initial impulse for *The West Wing*. In *The American President* Annette Bening got only a few fleeting scenes to prove that she could talk like Rosalind Russell. In *The West Wing*, Allison Janney got hours on end to prove that she could talk like Rosalind Russell, Irene Dunne, Jean Arthur, and Katharine Hepburn all sharing the one table at the Brown Derby.

Before *The West Wing* started I had laughed at Janney as the sluttish mother in *Drop Dead Gorgeous*, noticed her gangly pathos in *Primary Colors*, and had put together a mental collection of cameos that added up to a favorable impression; but the impression was the merest hint of the display of virtuosity she would unfold as C. J. Cregg in *The West Wing* over the course of years, and could give not even a token of its depth. When Danny brings the wrong goldfish to C.J.'s office and gets himself kissed at long last, it is one of the great love scenes in the American hall of heroic imagery, and when she mourns for her demented father, and seethes against the policy of affirmative action— one of the liberal values she is employed to favor—that has played a part in bringing his life to ruin, it is, on its quiet and contained level, great tragedy. Throughout the show, she can deploy that range of emotion because she has been given room. After the show ended she retained her new prestige and was more in demand than she had ever been before it started, but she was back to doing cameos, and on the right night, with the right accidental click on the remote, you can see her swapping quips with Charlie Sheen in a rerun of *Two and Half Men*. Wrong generation of Sheen. She ought to be swapping them with Charlie's father, and in our minds she still is.

Martin Sheen as President Bartlet brought such biting articulacy to his tightly argued humanist speeches in the first few shows that his role was enlarged, which gives you some idea of what a good actor he must be, because in real life, up to then, his political rhetoric functioned mainly as a means to register protest. Rather than climbing into the longest black limo in the White House motorcade, he could be more easily imagined being hoisted into the back of a police van during a demonstration. Similarly, as Allison Janney has charmingly explained to several journalists, she can't really talk as well as that: sometimes she had to ask what the technical terms in a given speech actually meant. The show's heroes and heroines are all given their stature by the words Sorkin gives them to say. It's an elementary point that should need no emphasizing, but it needs to be hammered home or the show's ranking as a creation might be placed too low. The principal Westwingers are all quick speakers, but they aren't making their stuff up. The best of them seem to have realized that their main job is to make sure the urge to act doesn't get in the way of the words. The late John Spencer, playing Bartlet's chief of staff Leo McGarry, looked a bit old fashioned because he could sometimes be caught gritting his teeth when the speech he was delivering had already gritted.

On the page, a Sorkin speech already includes most of

the timing required for its delivery. This remained true for the dialogue of *The West Wing* even after Sorkin left the show, having written, on his own, every episode of the first four seasons. From the fifth season onward, Sorkin, who was contending with the physical results of colliding with a dumper-load of mushrooms and cocaine, not only didn't write any further episodes, he didn't even watch them. But he had created a style, and his producer John Wells, as the new head man of the organization, took it from there.

The speeches that were handed to Josh Lyman (Bradley Whitford) and Donna Moss (Janel Moloney)—pages and pages of dialogue that William Powell and Myrna Loy would have slain for—were good enough to turn them into Romeo and Juliet. For any viewer the age of me or my wife, the only problem about watching and listening to the slow-burning romance of Josh and Donna was the high speed of what they said, often during long walking talks down corridors. (Luckily we had two keen-eared daughters smart enough to translate it.) But none of the quick talk would have seemed in keeping if the president had spoken like Eisenhower or George Bush. The tone and the pace are set by Jed Bartlet, which makes *The West Wing* an exemplary use of the charismatic central hero, a phenomenon which some stories can do without, but without which this story would be dead.

Jed Bartlet is an intellectual president. Previously in the twentieth century, there had been scarcely one of these. Theodore Roosevelt read everything, including, unfortunately, too many books about eugenics; Woodrow Wilson perhaps rated as a thinker; but FDR, though there wasn't much he couldn't understand—he even understood the atomic bomb, when the idea was eventually brought to him—was notable for applying his powers of reason more to everyday political detail than to the sweep of history: "The only thing we have to fear is fear itself" is more an advertising slogan than a thought. Harry Truman, still the most underrated of the modern presidents, had considerable book-learning, but it is a secret now because it was a secret then: he found it expedient to make himself sound ordinary. LBJ's intelligence was underrated because of his cornball manners; but he can hardly be thought of as one who lived by the light of reason. JFK's reputation for mental scope was largely constructed by those around him: it was Richard Nixon who could play the piano, but JFK got credentials as a music lover because Jackie sat him down in public to listen to Pablo Casals. Lately, Barack Obama published at least one good book which he actually wrote, but his idea of profundity was to announce that a vote for him would stop the ocean rising. All those real-life presidents were smart, but even with their reputations rolled together they don't add up to Jed Bartlet, who, in one of any number of illustrative scenes, gives us an account of exactly why developments in the cultivation of wheat present a decisive objection to Malthusian theories about imminent world starvation. President Bartlet started off as an economist at an exalted level, and has somehow managed to go on acquiring knowledge even while embroiled in the full time job of gaining political advancement. The only comparable presidential figure in American history is Lincoln, whose brilliance was confined to the English language. When Bartlet, after the accidental death of his beloved old secretary Mrs. Landingham, lingers in the church to unleash a defiant speech against God, he delivers it in Latin.

In other words, President Bartlet is really Aaron Sorkin himself, correctly intuiting that this is the way America, and indeed the whole free world, would like the occupant of the Oval Office to be: omniscient, energetic, an ethical giant, a poet king. The capacity to arouse a hankering for rule by royalty is probably built into the job, or anyway into the initial constitutional error which combined the administrative duties of the head of government with the symbolic duties of the head of state. In my lifetime I have seen only a few screen products in which actors imitate British royalty: Colin Firth played George VI in the battle against his own stammer; Helen Mirren played Elizabeth II overcoming her urge to seek seclusion in Balmoral after the Princess of Wales was killed; and Naomi Watts, Catherine Oxenburg, Serena Scott Thomas and several others all shared the task of helping to remind us that the Princess of Wales, in real life, was nothing like an actress. On the other hand, I have lost count of American screen treatments in which awe-stricken actors evoke the royal status of the president, or even of the vice president. I remember that Fredric March, in *Seven Days in May,* was a bit of a Bartlet when, armed with the wise constitutional provision by which an elected official is commander in chief of the armed forces, he stymied the usurpatory pretensions of Burt Lancaster as head of the Joint Chiefs. One thinks immediately of the *West Wing* scenes in which Bartlet, handicapped initially by his self-conscious awareness that he has seen no military service, makes a friend of head of the Joint Chiefs, Admiral Fitzwallace (John Amos), only to see him killed off in the Middle East convoy bombing which so nearly ends the life of Donna that Josh must fly to her hospital in Germany and once again, after what seems like a decade of unbearable delay, find himself not quite able to declare his love.

But one thinks of those scenes immediately only because *The West Wing* has taken the supremacy: it is our first frame of reference for thinking about the presidency. In *PT 109* Cliff Robertson was on his way to the White House. So was Robert Redford in *The Candidate:* though he was only running for senator, why else would he have nixed his sideburns except to seek supreme office? In 1988 there was a marvelous TV serial *Tanner,* jointly concocted by Robert Altman and Garry Trudeau, with Michael Murphy as an overqualified, and therefore unsuccessful, Democrat nominee. (*Tanner* might even have been Sorkin's direct inspiration for *The West Wing,* if it wasn't the movie *Thirteen Days.*) And so it goes on, all the way to the whole cluster of recent movies in which Morgan Freeman is the president; to the movie *The Contender,* in which Joan Allen was going to be the vice president; and to the plethora of TV shows including *Commander in Chief,* in which Geena Davis is the president; *Veep,* in which Julia Louis-Dreyfus reduces the vice president's political role to the farce which we all secretly think it is anyway; and *Madame Secretary*, in which Téa Leoni is secretary of state—minor royalty in her case, perhaps, but she looks the part, her lithe grace gaining in stature from not being chased by Jurassic raptors.

To look the part, even when the Terrorists have captured the White House and tied you to a railing down in the bunker while they murder your staff one by one so that you will give up the launch codes, you have to be classy, or know how to fake it. Martin Sheen is terrifically good at being classy: he can't make himself tall, but he knows just how to make himself look as if he has a connoisseur's respect for Yo Yo Ma's cello playing; or, even more impressive, for the moral stature of the African leader (Zakes Mokae) who has come begging for help in his war against the AIDS virus that is laying waste to his country. Almost every episode of *The West Wing* has a scene that qualifies for the title of best scene in the whole show, but most Wingnuts will agree that nothing quite equals the scene in which Toby Ziegler (Richard Schiff), pithily interpreting the technicalities for us as is his wont, explains just why the powerful drug companies are reluctant to hand over their antiviral product: the recipients will find it hard to self-administer, because the pills have to be taken at precise intervals. And why will that be a problem? Because nobody owns a watch. The pathos of the scene is made all the harder to forget because Schiff is so good at understatement. He just says the words. It's the mark of the Bartlet administration to just say the words, and of course it's the chief reason why the Bartlet administration is like nothing that has ever happened in real life, where everything that gets officially said has to be sold like a used car.

Above all, Bartlet's administration, in at least one crucial respect, is nothing like Bill Clinton's. There is no sex; except, early on, between Sam and the escort girl he saves from herself (yet another disarming performance from Lisa Edelstein); and not even Sam, strangely enough, tried to get it on with the token West Wing Republican Ainsley Hayes. But not so strange, because Emily Procter as Ainsley isn't there to be desirable—she can be that in *CSI Miami,* to which she eventually migrated, fitting so well into the sensual landscape that she sealed the relationship with botox—she's there to be a brilliant conservative antagonist for Bartlet's cluster of brilliant liberals. Sorkin's idea of a sexual encounter between adults is a protracted debate, usually with the female gaining the upper hand, like Beatrice talking scornful rings around Dante in Paradise. This rule isn't broken even by Bartlet's daughter Zoey (Elisabeth Moss) and his African American body-man Charlie Young (Dulé Hill), who are scarcely adults at all: they go to bed together, but it's almost as if that kind of fooling around is something that adolescents do before they grow up and start reading philosophy. Danny and C.J. have already talked themselves into a state of mutual obsession long before the wrong goldfish incident inspires their first kiss. In Bartlet's White House, from the sexual angle, nothing untoward will ever happen. In Bill Clinton's White House, something untoward resoundingly did.

Seen from the angle of, say, the Elysée Palace, Bartlet's White House might seem the more odd, because its ruling assumption is that the Bartlet marriage, though inevitably strained by the contest of two careers, is as secure as the house itself. In the world of fact, from FDR until now, roughly half of the American presidents have been unfaithful to their wives at some point, but in the world of fiction that possibility is seldom allowed to come up. *The West Wing* would have been a different show had it done so, and quite probably not a better one; although I can't have been the only male viewer to have wondered, early on, whether the depiction of the first lady, as played by Stockard Channing, might not have been designed to set up the possibility of Bartlet as a philandering successor to FDR, if not to JFK. Registering understandable impatience with his marriage to the job, she seemed also to be registering impatience with the United States, the Constitution and the world itself. (I hasten to add that Stockard Channing, with her Ida Lupino imitation in the spoof movie *The Big Bus,* gave one of the great parodic performances. Unfortunately some of her subsequent work suggests that she might still be on the bus.) Still, a Jed Bartlet with a sexual secret would have been regarded as un-American, and would therefore have never reached the network. The only secret Jed Bartlet has is the comparatively slight business of being subject to a case of multiple sclerosis whose paralytic side effects might induce him to black out in the situation room and inadvertently launch a nuclear strike against the Chinese navy, or the Russian army, or some little thing like that. The hiding of a potentially debilitating disease is a precedent set by JFK that Bartlet is allowed to follow. The precedent that JFK set by smuggling Marilyn Monroe into the White House is not one that would interest Bartlet. He is interested in every field of human endeavor except that. Why, then, do we find him so intensely human?

Mainly because he pays for his superior gifts with high anxiety. Where the rest of us might have a nagging conscience, he has an aching sense of responsibility. He knows he is the best man for his job because he is the best qualified for analysis and decision; but he can't be at ease in his role, because he knows history too well. Bartlet transcends the usual picture of the charismatic central figure because he shows at all times that he is not exercising irresponsible power. After his newly appointed personal physician is killed in the Middle East, he wants to level the whole area. He knows he can't. He doesn't want to accept advice about a "proportional response," but he knows he must. He has the quarrel with his advisers, and with himself, right there in front of us: in which lies the drama. Sorkin is inspiringly good at giving us a father figure and then proving that the father figure has, if not precisely feet of clay, then certainly a mind that suffers. In *The West Wing* the purity of language is unreal: network rules prevail and we never hear a dirty word. Nor does anyone, not even a writer, ever really talk that well. But there is realism about the way reasoned conclusions are reached.

In that regard, the most advanced stroke of realism in the show is the way that not even the brilliant Bartlet can function without hearing other voices. Those of us who hanker for a father figure should remember that if he existed then he would need a father figure too. Though Bartlet is a mighty chess player, *The West Wing* is a pretty good shot at fighting off the romanticism by which the central guru can understand the whole board at a glance. In *I, Claudius* Augustus sometimes didn't know what was really going on, but he didn't know that he didn't know. Bartlet incarnates Camus's definition of democracy as the system built and maintained by those who know that they don't know everything. Romantic longings will always tempt us to reject that principle, especially when it comes to the business of admiring a screen hero. Playing Julius Caesar in the TV series *Rome*, Ciarán Hinds was fully as good as Rex Harrison in *Cleopatra* at being the smartest emperor ever. The consequence, alas, was the same in both cases: when Rex Harrison's Caesar got assassinated, it left us with nothing but Burton and Taylor very believably being fatally bad for each other, and when Ciarán Hinds departed from *Rome*, so did the center of interest. It is almost impossible to portray a political hero without romanticizing

him. In *The West Wing* Aaron Sorkin came close to man-
aging it, making a questioning, troubled intellect seem a
desirable quality for a politician to have, even in an era
where the sound bite had come to power. (In *The West
Wing* there are not yet any tweets, but the blogs are already coarsening the language of politics.) With its probing, dialectical treatment of every liberal issue, including
race—one thinks with special fondness of Edward James
Olmos as Justice Roberto Mendoza, Bartlet's Latino nominee for the Supreme Court—*The West Wing* reminded
the world that America had intellectual capacity behind
its economic muscle, and surely helped prepare the way
for Barack Obama's election. If Sorkin had gone on to
do a show about the first Jewish president, he might have
changed history; but he had other projects in mind.

Sweet Faces Speak Poetry

IF SORKIN, IN *The West Wing*, was racing on the crown of the asphalt, in his later ventures *Studio 60 on the Sunset Strip* and *The Newsroom* he has spent a lot of time on the grass. In motor racing terminology "on the grass" means you have mistimed the corner and are bouncing and skidding along in one of the run-off areas at the side of the track, hoping not to get stuck in a gravel trap. The metaphor is perhaps a bit too strict to be used in the appreciation of Sorkin's later shows. My elder daughter Claerwen has done a dedicated Sorkinista's job of making me watch them several times each until enough virtues emerge to make me less confident about pointing out their vices. But I still think that *Studio 60*, in particular, is a misapplication of the body of expertise that Sorkin built up while in charge of those first four seasons of *The West Wing*. Wanting more of the same, we perhaps had the wrong expectations of him when he moved on; but it seems equally likely that he had the wrong expectations of himself. He thought he could transfer the same density and complexity of treatment from the world of politics to the world of comedy. But the world of comedy can't take the weight, because it is full of people who, far from fighting against their own histrionic tendencies, give in to them. It's serious, but not in a serious way: and is thus a lot harder to treat dramatically. I worked in the field of television comedy for twenty years myself, and I'd be the first to say that the day is full of vital decisions, but they're not the same as deciding whether to send in the Marines, or even deciding whether to pardon a turkey.

The inside story of the *Studio 60* comedy show might as well be the inside story of *Saturday Night Live* transferred from New York to Los Angeles. The on-screen show-runners, Danny and Matt, played by Bradley Whitford from *The West Wing* and Matthew Perry from *Friends* (impossible not to think of their origins in each case), are essentially Lorne Michaels split into two, so that he can argue with himself. Their arguments fizz and snap all around the building, but the basic Thomas Schlamme directorial device of *The West Wing*—a Steadicam dialogue conducted while

the protagonists walk at high speed down the corridor—
works less well when there are no corridors. (In *The News-room* the anomaly is even worse, because the walking talks happen in an open-plan office, with everybody else pretending not to listen, like those other people drinking coffee in *Friends*.) This technical handicap would have mattered less, however, had the supposedly comic players in the show actually been funny. None of them is, except perhaps Alex Dwyer (Simon Helberg), who does appropriately crazed imitations of Tom Cruise and Nicolas Cage. Fatally, Harriet Hayes, the key character of the enchantingly stately young woman who is also enchantingly amusing—i.e., the Gilda Radner persona in the *Saturday Night Live* lineup—is, as played by Sarah Paulson (trapped in the role, I fear), more winsome than stately, and no more amusing than Ivana Trump. Matt's thwarted love for her has driven him to drugs, but Danny has done much better with his boss Jordan McDeere (Amanda Peet), although in true Sorkin style it takes Danny almost a whole season of twenty-two episodes to find out where his heart lies. (One of the many true lessons from classic Hollywood that Sorkin took in with his mother's milk is that we must first love the lovers before they love each other.) Indeed Amanda

Peet is the one who delivers the Gilda Radner thrill, partly because her refined glamour is multiplied by her character's position of power, thereby putting her on the pedestal which Sorkin obviously thinks is the appropriate position for any heroine in whom one of his smart heroes is interested. But by the time we have figured that out, the casting of the show-within-the-show has ceased to matter. One wonders only briefly why the show's supposedly cute and cuddly small male Tom Jeter (Nate Corddry) is given no proof of humor beyond his capacity to dress up as a bee. Or was it an ant? What matters about him is that his brother is captured in Afghanistan, thereby giving *Studio 60 on the Sunset Strip* an opportunity to do what it has been longing to from the start: turn back into *The West Wing*. Immediately the studio green room turns into the White House situation room; there is a high-ranking military attaché ordering the resident beautiful female lawyer (played by the pitilessly arousing Kari Matchett) to cease negotiating for the hostage's release; the clock is ticking in a deadly countdown; and all that remains to happen is for President Bartlet to come charging in and take over.

Actually, all that remained to happen was for the show to die. After so blatant an unveiling of its true yearnings, it could barely stay credible until the unmourned close of its only season. It was a worthy effort, with a lot of clever talk; and both my daughters still like to go through it in search of its many minor pleasures; but there were too few major ones, and Sorkin never really got the show on the road. He looked as if he might be on the grass for keeps.

He did better with *The Newsroom*, which, instead of being about theater, is really about news, and therefore is practically about politics, the field which best answers Sorkin's theatrical instincts. My whole family has binge-watched all three seasons at least once each, and Claerwen finds it an honorable development in Sorkinism. So, after a long pondering, do I, but I still think that the key man is the weak link. It isn't the fault of the actor, Jeff Daniels, that he gives a matinee idol's improbably distinguished profile to Will McAvoy, the anchorman he is impersonating; but it is the fault of the writing, directing, and the whole shebang that McAvoy is given the ennobled importance (it's that royal thing again) which America has traditionally awarded to news anchors from Huntley, Brinkley, and Cronkite onward, with all of them revered as if they were Ed Murrow reborn. Since Sorkin's truest gift is for analytical idealism, not satire, there is no point faulting *The Newsroom* for making its protagonists so concerned with keeping the news clean. But we could have used more indication that there have been striking instances in the real world of the American newsrooms deliberately getting the news wrong. McAvoy might have at least referred, in his off-screen banter, to the way that CBS News, with the great Dan Rather fully implicated, cooked the facts about George W. Bush's avoidance of war service in Vietnam. CBS was swindled with a falsified document, but it stuck with the swindle, and Rather kept plugging the lie right until the end, which turned out to be his. Those of us who had never thought him to be all that impressive anyway—he never seemed to realize how phony he looked in a flak jacket—managed to hold back our tears when he finally headed off to a well-paid marginalization on cable, but wry thoughts of William Hurt's actorish anchor in James Brooks's excellent movie *Broadcast News* were hard to quell.

Sorkin quelled them. The plotline of *The Newsroom*'s second season deals throughout with how the team talks itself into transmitting false news about the Marines using Sarin gas, but the false news is an honest mistake. The question of ambitious wrongdoing scarcely comes up. McAvoy and his roomful of clever colleagues spend hours on end agonizing in true *West Wing* style about how their good-ness failed, without even raising the possibility that there might be such a thing as evil. Finally it hits them in the face when a newly hired colleague is revealed as the perfidious culprit. He has to be an interloper; and of course he can't possibly be the man behind the onscreen desk. We can't expect McAvoy to find within himself any possibility that he might warp the truth to his advantage: he's not the type. But McAvoy is meant to have a brain as well as a person-ality, and human faults are meant to be within his mental grasp. Instead he is the last to suspect instead of the first; and at no point in any of the show's twenty-five episodes does he even begin to consider that the on-air language of even the most honest anchor might be spurious anyway, since the demands of the twenty-four-hour news cycle are that everything must be made to sound important even when it isn't. *The Newsroom* thus finds itself in the anoma-lous position of frittering away the main advantage that a long-form TV show has over a movie: room to search souls. *Broadcast News* managed to nail an issue in a couple of hours that *The Newsroom* barely scratched in a whole season. What if the anchor is a fraud?

Since the show ended, a national news anchor has been

caught shyly boasting the same sort of action-packed back-story that Hillary Clinton cooked up for herself after landing in Sarajevo "under sniper fire." To improve the facts is a human temptation that a worker in news must suppress, not be without. When not occupied with putting himself into profile, McAvoy unstoppably speaks speeches, of such fluency that we must struggle to notice how he is a robot calibrated to operate only at the speed of the news cycle, and never less: when condescending to listen to the opinion of reverent underlings, he still rewards them with chunks of the Constitution compressed into epigrams. Luckily for us, he is surrounded by characters who bear a stronger resemblance to human beings, although even they show signs of having been assembled from standard components. McAvoy's boss Charlie Skinner (Sam Waterston) is a tower of scotch-pickled wisdom until he finally drops dead, perhaps so that the actor can get back to *Law and Order* and continue being a tower of wisdom there. Charlie is a television perennial, the wise one that you can find wearing pointed ears in reruns of *Star Trek* and will find again under the name of Saul Berenson in *Homeland*. (Glowering knowledgeably behind them all is Ben Bradlee, as played by Jason Robards in *All the President's Men*, a performance so riveting that Bradlee is rumored to have copied it in real life afterward.) Charlie didn't need Obi Wan Kenobi to be inspired by: the guru figure has been cropping up since the earliest days of Hollywood, where every studio chief looked with favor on the idea of a veteran male screen character who embodied the sum of human wisdom. Scott Fitzgerald thought the wise man might be Irving Thalberg, and wrote a hagiographical text about him, *The Last Tycoon*.

Sorkin is saturated by a heritage of stock characters, which he transports to the level of originality by making them articulate. Jane Fonda as the proprietress Leona Lansing plays the Nancy Marchand role from *Lou Grant*. Furnished with aphoristic dialogue worthy of Congreve, she makes a plausible exemplar of the proposition that somebody with enough money could be ready to subsidize the truth, as if it were an art museum: irony-prone onlookers have suggested that she might have borrowed her altruism from her ex-husband Ted Turner. I personally, in all my own altruism, think the show caught a lucky break when it couldn't get Marisa Tomei to play executive producer MacKenzie McHale and got Emily Mortimer instead. McAvoy needs a Cambridge-educated antelope to fall for, and Marisa

Tomei would have been (here I cough discreetly) too sexy. Speaking of sex, Olivia Munn as the ultrabright economics anchor Sloan Sabbith is two different kinds of dynamite, and from the visual angle would be enough all by herself to raise the perennially vexed question about eye candy, which I hereby propose to treat, although very briefly. After all, I am pledged to run these remarks past the women of my family, and they still want to know why I, at my age, and in my depleted state of health, sobbed aloud when Zoe Barnes got pushed under the train.

Sloan Sabbith has two Ph.D.'s and the face of a wicked angel. Sorkin, a romantic idealist, has always been glad to present us with a female character whose beauty is rivaled only by her brains. In *The American President* Annette Bening completed her enslavement of Michael Douglas when she unexpectedly spoke French to the French ambassador: a dollop of cream for the key lime pie. If a female character is meant to be enticing even against her will, the combination of oomph and smarts is an enabling device for the character's creator: Sloan's two Ph.D.s legitimize her bewitching eyes and her figure fit for the swimsuit issue of *Sports Illustrated*. But we can't mention any of that stuff, because this is America, whose culture insists that the love object not be objectified, and that love, a thing of the spirit, must transcend lust, a thing of the mere body. Nietzsche thought that sexuality influenced the whole human personality all the way to the top of the mind, but Nietzsche was a German fruitcake. The matter could be debated endlessly, but the debate tends to reach the screen only in the form of casting. In Britain the BBC leads the way toward satisfying the supposed demands of antisexist justice by filling the police station with ordinary-looking female cops and making sure that the only female cop who is supposed to look like a heartbreaker gets defenestrated in the second episode. As a result, the ITV cop shows have a better chance in the export market: Helen Mirren as Detective Jane Tennison in *Prime Suspect* spent seven years being a hit all over the world. She's a fine actress, even better than Queen Elizabeth II at holding regal sway, but anyone who didn't think Mirren's timeless sexual appeal was part of her impact would be dreaming. In Britain, though, such casting now counts as a rare event, and even as a retrograde step.

The Americans, despite agonies of ideological guilt—they are under constant pressure to believe that pulchritude is a social construct, instead of a divine caprice—still find themselves obliged to obey the ancient and perhaps accursed Hollywood rule of putting attractive females on screen wherever possible, and especially if the character is supposed to be one. Alas for all enemies of sexism, that rule entails a further rule, which is that the eye candy, once in position on screen, should not be casually dispensed with. I myself am living proof of the fact that a male viewer can be well past the age of misbehavior and still lose his heart to a pretty face, at least to the point of missing her when the plot wipes her out. Quite apart from Kate Mara's collision with the Washington Metrorail system, I found it hard to take when Krysten Ritter disappeared from *Breaking Bad*. (Luckily she popped up again a few weeks later as a frenemy of the headliner in *Veronica Mars:* in my dotage I find that the screen stories, as I shuffle the boxes in which they are contained, tend to blend together, like a Cowes regatta sucked into the Sargasso.) But Sorkin has never needed to be convinced that a pretty face should catch our imagination even before it starts unspooling aphorisms from La Rochefoucauld. His high place in the long-form television world looked like proof in itself that a screen story depends on an ample supply of courtly love. But it only looked like it, because in *The Wire* romance was dead from the start.

City of the Dead

FROM THE FIRST GLANCE, the mise-en-scène of *The Wire* was *Waterworld* with the water let out, *Mad Max* come back from the future, *The Battle of Algiers* crossed with *Black Orpheus*, or the back streets of *Robocop* where only a metal man dares go. But no, it was just a hopeless stretch of residential Baltimore emptied of jobs, amenities, and civilization before being filled up with black males, not one of whom looked likely to be a candidate for the presidency anytime soon. Instead, they had their minds on drugs: everyone who wasn't using was dealing. When you got into it, however, it soon emerged that Stringer Bell (Idris Elba) would have been an ideal candidate for the presidency, if his naturally fine mind had not been wasted from his childhood by the unremitting violence of his surroundings. Imagine Stringer telling you that a vote for him would stop the rising ocean. From him, you would believe it. That's the impression the show gives from the start: waste. Later on, the show-runner David Simon published his opinion that there should be no criminal prosecutions relating to drugs unless an innocent party got hurt. He meant that the war against drugs was unwinnable. But he scarcely needed to put us on formal notice: the show conveys no other message. This is the Waste Land; and in its beginning is its end. Nothing can fix this. Entertainment never looked more bleak.

But entertaining it was. I saw my first episode of *The Wire* when I was in Australia, and I flew home to England already programmed to buy a box as soon as I landed. The first character to catch my eye and ear was Jimmy McNulty, played by Dominic West, the Eton alumnus who came to world prominence through a switch of accent and a plunge into the unknown. In a context where most of the cops, like most of the crooks and victims, are black, there was no compulsion to make the hero white except to avoid the same ratings as a rerun of *Shaft* on a junk channel in the early morning. As things turned out, *The Wire* never did get the ratings, just as it never got the awards; but it was an instantaneous and enduring *succès d'estime* with an intelligent audience worldwide, and if my own case counts, then that appreciation had something to do with gratitude for seeing the question of color treated with such bravery, which is to say, with such a lack of sentimentality. The leading outlaws in the show—Avon Barksdale, Marlo Stanfield, Omar Little, Proposition Joe, and the whole bunch of lethal adolescents jostling to replace them—aren't dumber than McNulty: it's just that most of them didn't learn anything in school, because the school was just another branch of needle park. McNulty's colleague Bunk Moreland (Wendell Pierce), who did learn something, makes a fitting, smart-talking friend: they get drunk together very well, and the time they visit the crime scene together and say nothing but "fuck" every time they find a piece of evidence is the one scene in modern television that everyone in the family can quote if allowed to. (My wife, normally resistant to the putative charm of foul-mouthed male dialogue, laughed her head off.) But McNulty, if we ourselves are white, is our representative traveler down into the nightmare: as Dante says of himself in *Inferno* XXVIII, he stays in the ditch to watch the ruined people, how they spend their time.

McNulty's story on its own could have made a series: as a highly believable magnet for women, Ted Hughes with a gun, he could have sustained a plotline in which he did nothing between making arrests except get his rocks off in various directions. But part of the show's lavishness is that McNulty is only a single thread in the sad tapestry we see before us as we go in. It looks like chaos, but the chaos proves to have a pattern: the drug-runners own the corners, and every corner is a center of a circularity, where the supply arrives from the upper level of distributors and leaves again in the hands of the consumers. Somewhere at the top of the upper level is a kingpin, monitoring his own system while he prepares himself against incursion from other kingpins.

It's a whole society, except that it's entirely antisocial. Very soon the show works the magic trick of any successful myth, and convinces you that the phantasmagoria you see in front of you is real and inevitable, and that the major characters are aspects of your own complex personality. I have no trouble seeing myself as Idris Elba. It's as easy as seeing myself as Denzel Washington. (I speak as the kind of Denzel fan who watches *Man on Fire* again every time it comes on screen.) Stringer Bell has beauty; grace; brains; energy. Why, this man is me! So of *course* he has to kill a few people here and there. Just as long as he continues with his programme of self-education in business practice, which will surely save him from the cycle of death. One of the show's many triumphs is that we are so thoroughly convinced that Stringer Bell is an invulnerable mastermind right up until the moment when he gets blown away, and that he gets blown away so casually, as in one of those real-life tragedies that make real life so hard to bear. On the other hand the trash scavenger Bubbles (Andre Royo) lives forever, though he has no powers to defend himself. We have art in order not to perish from the truth, as Nietzsche said in a notebook: a remark that Camus cites in *The Myth of Sisyphus* when telling us how to survive in an absurd world. Nietzsche, Camus, and Bubbles, *The Wire*'s philosopher with a shopping cart full of scrap.

The *terra nullius* of *The Wire* is an absurd world that works. At the cost of occasionally killing even someone like Stringer, and of eventually quite possibly killing everybody, the drug world continues indefinitely. Its plan of organization, however, is defined with clarity; and the plan is what fascinates, to the extent that the second season seems comparatively negligible when it moves away from the drug-dealing areas to the docks and puts the action in the hands of a few corrupt white stevedores and standard imported Greek and Balkan heavies. There aren't enough black people. A few containers get parked profitably in the wrong place; a few foreign cars get heisted; but that's as fascinating as the skulduggery ever gets, although some might say that the Port Authority officer Beadie Russell (Amy Ryan), who finds thirteen corpses in one container, is fascinating enough to make up the difference. Back in the days of *On the Waterfront*, the corrupt union bosses took a percentage of everything that moved in and out of New York. On the Baltimore waterfront they are taking a piece of a diminished traffic. The real action is back in town, to which, thankfully, we are frequently referred in subplots during the second season; and from the third season onward the various narrative lines are all directly concerned with the main event, which is how the black people live in a postindustrial residential landscape, and how easily they die. The docks are interesting enough, but it's in the houses that we are faced with a more complex and inexhaustibly interesting code of misbehavior.

And that's what we get: a code. The show makes the move that will ensure its greatness when it takes us into the network of expertise by which the drug hustlers work their sad supremacy. The key is in the communications between the bosses and the minions on the corners. The messages are coded. Listening in to the phones of the miscreants (the show ought rightly to be called *The Tap*, not *The Wire*, but let that pass), our basement full of cops have to crack the code or lose the battle. Lester Freamon (Clarke Peters) is our mastermind in charge, but detective Ronald "Prez" Pryzbylewski (Jim True-Frost), a white guy of Polish background with an established rep as a violent klutz, is the one who comes up with the goods, almost as much to his own surprise as ours. The code depends on the dialer touching or skipping certain buttons on the touch-tone dial. It's simple to use but hard to figure out. The smart move of the script at this point is to follow the figuring out. Luckily the code, though complicated enough to be plausible, is just simple enough to allow this treatment. The result is screen magic. Almost always, elsewhere in screen history, to show the characters solving a technical puzzle is a formula for screen death, or else the matter is fudged, resulting in screen stupidity. One need only think of the 1980 mini-series *Oppenheimer*, in which the script avoids both the physics and the engineering of the atomic bomb, leaving us with nothing but a character analysis of the hero. Nor do any of the television or movie accounts of the World War II code-breaking at Bletchley Park come anywhere near making a drama out of the problem: they make their drama out of the characters. (Take a look at what Charles Dance has been given to do in *The Imitation Game*—grit his teeth and keep growling that the code must be cracked by dawn—and you get some idea of just how grateful he must have been for his long and manifold role as Tywin Lannister in *Game of Thrones*). Between them, Robert Harris, who wrote the novel *Enigma*, and Tom Stoppard, who wrote the screenplay, get close to transmitting the Bletchley thrill, but they can do so only by developing the subject into a spy story about how Saffron Burrows and Kate Winslet crack the secret of the Katyn massacre. Nobody cracks the actual Enigma code except by looking tense. They might as well be sucking pencils. Not even Stoppard, who has a mind in the Bletchley league, can show a mind at work. An image just can't do it, unless the puzzle is almost within our grasp.

In *The Wire* we see Prez make the leap. It's pure screen drama. Fittingly, Prez has another such moment at the end of the final season, when, in his new persona as a successful schoolteacher—having been useful in the fight against the drug lords was what put him on the road to fulfillment— he realizes that a treasured pupil is not going to escape the drug world after all, but is being sucked back down to doom. Along with the bid by the white "Tommy" Carcetti (Aiden Gillen) to replace a black mayor, education is one of the big themes in the later chapters. The good guys, like Prez, put every effort into it, but they can't win the young-sters away from the bad guys, because really there is no good and bad, there is just the system. An even bigger theme is even more depressing: the black senior policeman Major Howard ("Bunny") Colvin (Robert Wisdom), defi-nitely a good guy, gets the impossibly bold idea of estab-lishing his district as a zone where drugs are effectively legal as long as the gunfire stops. For a while it seems to work, but that's just why it can't last. So the total effect of the show is entirely pessimistic: a rare event in American culture. The show-runners are essentially saying that in the postindustrial landscape, with no real work for anyone to do, the black minority becomes the majority only through being locked into its depressed status as a subclass. David Simon went far enough toward deserving our applause for such an unflinching view of circumstances determining behavior. We can't ask him, in his screen work, to raise the question of whether there might be such a thing as an in-dividual choice independent of determinism. It should be noted, however, that in his off-screen work, he did so, if only at one point: in his real-life book of reportage *The Corner* he brings on a young black character who is so gifted at legitimate business that he looks like breaking out of the deadly system which has brought all his contemporaries to early ruin. Having built up a bank balance of money legitimately earned, the character is sufficiently excited by achievement; but he eventually takes a taste of the poison anyway, and likes it. So down he goes into the same pit as everybody else.

In my crowded memory of the show, which I might not have time to sit through again while I yet live, two things stand out even in a maelstrom of outstanding things: the androgynous young enforcer Snoop (Felicia Pearson), who shoots people simply because she likes it, and Lester's discovery of the nailed-up houses in which the bodies have been left to rot in their thin dusting of quicklime. Of *The Wire*, so full of life—who wouldn't like to get drunk with Bunk?—the abiding image is of a City of the Dead. It's all so cruelly pointless that it makes you long for a real crime.

Breaking Understandably Bad

REAL CRIME WAS LARGELY MISSING from *Treme,* the misguided attempt by *The Wire*'s creators to take new territory. It wasn't their fault that the factual setup was so short of juice. Unless you were an ultraorthodox climate change believer, there was no way of blaming the Bush administration for the hurricane that flooded New Orleans, so there was nobody to blame except the New Orleans administration that failed to keep up the levees; which would have meant blaming black people with a specificity that not even *The Wire* had dared to do. For understandable reasons it was deemed preferable to show us how people in the Treme (pronounced to rhyme with "away") district went on playing excellent jazz while the city recovered, or failed to. Unfortunately, even for people who love jazz as much as I do, the music has traditionally never held the screen. As Clint Eastwood inadvertently proved with his movie *Bird*, not even the life of Charlie Parker can be made to look interesting by an actor with a sax sticking out of his mouth. (To be fair to Eastwood, though, his 1984 movie *Tightrope* had some nice stretches of sweet old jazz in the streets of New Orleans; but a few minutes at a time was plenty.) In *Treme*, Wendell Pierce, this time called Antoine instead of Bunk, is there again from *The Wire*, but although he's lovable even when pretending to play a trombone, he would be more so if he said "fuck" instead. I like watching John Goodman venting his scorn of corrupt authority—it's like watching an airship emerging from its hangar, a tremendous combination of grace and volume— but he's better being a temporary president in *The West Wing* while Bartlet awaits the rescue of his kidnapped daughter. Or so I thought as I went gently to sleep, regularly nudged by Lucinda, who thought the show was pretty good. But she's a civil servant who knows a lot about housing, and the housing problems of post-Katrina New Orleans left me indifferent. I needed a villain. Give me real crime, not social circumstances.

Real crime was meant to be awarded epic status in *Boardwalk Empire*, but the show faced unbeatable competition even as it was being born. *The Sopranos* had already cornered the market in the fascination of an alternative outlaw universe, and *The Wire*'s black outlaws, with both feet in criminality, had somehow outdistanced the whole tradition of mob movies, whose white inhabitants were hampered by having one foot in respectability. A third factor arises from the question of whether Steve Buscemi, who stars as Enoch "Nucky" Thompson, is credible as a poised crime lord. He looks like a poised crime lord's raving mad subordinate; although admittedly that impression might arise from one's lingering memory of his arrival at screen prominence in a Coen Brothers context, where almost everyone looks insane. (The Coen Brothers can make you wonder if even George Clooney is quite all there.) Wasn't Buscemi closer to being himself when, in *The Sopranos,* after a couple of episodes of striving to look normal, he reverted to homicidal weirdness? An unfair question to ask about an actor, perhaps, because the whole business of an actor is not to get stuck in a single self; but Buscemi invited it every time he bared his teeth, so clearly designed for biting the head off a live chicken. Leaving questions of casting aside, however, the viewer who wants to be absorbed by the show is still stuck with the problem that Nucky's burgeoning organization burgeons to little purpose and with not much in the way of planning. We need to see the criminal mastermind's superiority as a strategist. Even Tony Soprano gives us that: it's how we know he's picking up tips when he watches History Channel documentaries about Rommel. You get that even in *The Borgias,* where the aging Roderigo Borgia (Jeremy Irons), while arthritically reveling in his title as Pope Alexander VI and in the Vatican's lavish supply of aristocratic young women, revels even more in explaining to his son Cesare (François Arnaud) that if the French army can be detained in Naples, the Neapolitan army can advance on Paris. Or is it the Nepalese army advancing on Pasadena? Whatever, this is the thing that Roderigo is best at and that Cesare will inherit: a sense for the mechanism of power. For dramatic purposes, it has to sound intricate even if it isn't. From Buscemi's Nucky Thompson you get almost none of that. Nucky has interesting relationships. His handsome but blundering brother Eli (Shea Whigham) is a rich source of embarrassment. Nucky has commendably complex feelings for his decent wife Margaret (Kelly Macdonald, that nice maid from *Gosford Park*). But Nucky's relationships are more interesting than he is, and we get little sense of what he is out to build, except perhaps a longer boardwalk. He makes moves to expand his bootlegging operation. The other hoodlums make moves to stop him. Head 'em off at the pass!

Roderigo and Cesare of *The Borgias*, their mobility confined to the speed of a horse, might envy *Boardwalk Empire*'s supply of vintage cars and machine guns but would be astounded by little else. The two shows ask to be linked because the set is the most eloquent protagonist in each case. The Borgia ambience looks as good as a panorama by Pinturicchio, and the Atlantic City boardwalk is a triumph of nostalgiaville art direction. But when you get down to the level of personnel, *Boardwalk Empire* is thin on people. Back from the war and lethally desensitized, the enforcer-for hire Jimmy Darmody (Michael Pitt) is a scary invention. Another war casualty, Jack Huston (Richard Harrow) is even scarier, having left half his face behind somewhere in France before returning to America as the remorseless dispenser of certain death. (Every crime show needs its own Terminator, but the idea is subject to the law of diminishing returns.) The story is weakened, however, through being staffed with walking wounded to run the office, as if the man in charge were insufficiently interesting. Hence the viewer longs for the gangster movies of an earlier day. In the old Richard Wilson movie *Al Capone*,

Rod Steiger did some of his most terrifying work, almost as if the man who took over Chicago were a slightly over-weight actor making shapes with his mouth as he blasted his way to center stage. And Ray Danton in the title role of Budd Boetticher's *The Rise and Fall of Legs Diamond* at least had physical style. Examples could be multiplied (the diminutive Mickey Rooney filled the screen as *Baby Face Nelson*), but it wouldn't be fair to Buscemi, whose role is simply underwritten. Nucky isn't present as a mind. As a result, we are left with an expensive heap of evidence that décor and action aren't enough.

Sometimes, in a movie, they are, or almost. Martin Scorsese, who directed the pilot, was an informing pres-ence behind the conception of *Boardwalk Empire*. Scorsese had proved with *Casino* that a shapeless story about rob-bers robbing each other could be at least partly redeemed by lovely slow motion shots of a Vegas bombing in which the poker chips float like colored snowflakes. But a TV show is never strong when it reminds you of how a movie made the same motif more beautiful; and Scorsese might have done more to note that the deadly taciturnity of the *Boardwalk* character who is least like one of his—Lucky Luciano, played by Vincent Piazza with a dead pan that could not be duplicated by Joe Pesci unless he was calmed down by Novocain—was the way to go, toward the sinisterly normal and away from the rococo picturesque. We need to be looking at a man in the middle who represents us in all our frightening secret power. Bernard Berenson said that Raphael reflects back to us the classicism of our yearnings.

Whether the antihero of *Breaking Bad* gives us back to ourselves is a question much discussed in my family. Lucinda sat the whole thing through with me and agreed perhaps too readily with my laughing suggestion that cooking crystal meth might have been one of the ways I could have gone; but my wife gave up watching, unable, much to my relief, to find the character plausible. Perhaps her opinion was a tribute to Britain's National Health Service, which ensures that no man stricken with a terminal illness need find a way of raising a quick few million dollars.

I found him plausible but dull. Failed chemists in America no doubt turn into drug overlords every day, but do they walk around in their underpants with their mouths open? It was that last part that set me nodding. Even my granddaughter gives me credit for the work that goes into my Benedict Cumberbatch impersonation: it's quite a strain on the corners of the mouth, pulling them down like that without using your fingers. But nobody gave me credit for my impersonation of Walter White, as played by Bryan Cranston. I would keep my mouth sagging open for ten minutes at a time but nobody gave me an Emmy. I should be more reverent, because the show was a huge hit: a legitimate source of pride for AMC, for Netflix, and for its creator, Vince Gilligan. Cranston, who had to outdo Spencer Tracy in transforming himself over time from mild to monstrous, was much praised for carrying the show, along with Anna Gunn as his wife, Skyler, bravely adjusting herself to the realization that her husband is a lying head case, as so many wives must.

After he is cheated out of a fortune by his unscrupulous science partner, Walter settles for an unspectacular career as a mere teacher, but when he is diagnosed with terminal cancer he realizes that his family will be left impoverished, so he breaks bad. He breaks understandably bad. But the criminal activity he opts to join is one that will inevitably damage people by the thousands. I found him hard to sympathize with even when he was reduced to his underpants, and I speak as someone who has done unspeakable things to stay in business: I once voluntarily interviewed the Spice

Girls. Luckily White has a brother-in-law, the DEA agent Hank Schrader, played by Dean Norris, who is marvelous at inhabiting the mental territory somewhere in between implacable detective and plodding knucklehead. Eventually he will be White's nemesis, but it takes him five seasons to get there. Another plus is the secretive drugs mastermind Gus Fring (Giancarlo Esposito), who proves that a black criminal kingpin can be as smart as Stringer Bell and still live. Or he almost proves it: in the end he presents us with one of the most stunning images in all the box set dramas when he walks toward us through a doorway with one side of his head missing. There is also Saul Goodman (Bob Odenkirk), a fast-talking shyster with bad taste in ties who looked set from the start to have his own series one day, as Frazier did after his first few speeches in *Cheers*. These subsidiary *Breaking Bad* characters are worth remembering when you question your own lingering impression that the show is underpopulated. It seems that way when you are bored by Walter's transformation or don't want to face it; or else you don't want to face your memories of his apprentice cook, Jesse Pinkman, played by Aaron Paul as the most unbearable punk since the one Clint Eastwood blew away in *Dirty Harry*. (I should name the actor, Andrew Robinson: it wasn't his fault that whole cinemas erupted like a Nuremberg rally when a slug from Harry's cannon took him out.)

Unfortunately, from my viewpoint, nobody blew away Jesse Pinkman before my patience was exhausted. Lucinda, who quite liked him, told me to stop being irrational, but I would put a cushion over my face rather than watch those unnaturally perfect teeth bared at me again. This was probably a triumph of acting, but still: there are things you don't want to see twice. Why Walter didn't upend his rebarbative assistant into a vat of bubbling acid was a mystery, and a bigger mystery was why the kid attracted the affections of Jane Margolis, played by Krysten Ritter in all her witty beauty. The latter mystery didn't last long, because she OD'd, and was helped along to death by Walter. I could just about put up with the loss of cheesecake, but I thought the show's texture could ill afford to lose her character, which had been light and quick: qualities otherwise sorely missing from the script, even when Saul was in full spiel. Still, perhaps it wasn't that kind of story; although it didn't seem to mind turning into a bad action movie at the end, when Walter wiped out the enemy with, guess what, a remote-controlled machine gun. He was supposed to be a chemist, not an ordnance engineer, and anyway we had seen the remote-controlled gun in the highly unnecessary Bruce Willis–Richard Gere remake of *The Jackal*, where it had already looked more than enough like a desperate plot device. With a TV drama as with any movie, it's always a bad sign when the image that flares into your head is of a bunch of tired writers listlessly shuffling their memories of scenes they've seen before.

Gilligan almost ditched the *Breaking Bad* project when he heard that HBO was going to make *Weeds*. He would have been wrong to do so—hundreds of millions of dollars wrong, and in show business you can't get more wrong than that—but there is a case for *Weeds* being the better product. It has a better subject, simply because the central figure is a law-abiding woman, not a law-abiding man, turning criminal in order to cope with adversity: we don't expect it from a woman. (Perhaps it is patronizing of us not to.) In *Breaking Bad*, Walter copes with lack of money by dispensing chemical danger to thousands of people. In *Weeds*, Nancy copes with lack of money by doing nothing worse than growing the soft and fragrant high that got so many of us through our belated adolescence, back there when the guitar licks of Jefferson Airplane floated sweetly over a crowded field of smoke. In fact Mary-Louise Parker looks a bit like Grace Slick. I soon got past my *idée fixe* that Parker was really the girlfriend Josh might have married instead of Donna. In *The West Wing* she was just another knockout Sorkin female highbrow with a fistful of Ph.D.s, but in *Weeds* she copes in the womanly way that so many of us fatherless ones learned to admire in our youth, although it tended to scare us in perpetuity by just the degree that we felt compelled to admire it. A lasting tribute to the female show-runner Jenji Kohan, Nancy is a heroic figurehead for womanly competence, a Florence Nightingale with incense in her lamp. In the course of seven seasons she gets through three husbands (one of them a DEA agent) and leaves every male in the cast looking like an appendage. The show is vast in emotional scope and I still haven't finished watching it, but nor have I quite dealt with its basic proposition that integrity can be maintained in a criminal context. Would the story work at all, if it paid due attention to the insistence by John Phillips that pot was the gateway to hard drugs and grim death? Phillips loved the sweet music too (as a member of the Mamas and Papas he created more than his share of it) but he wasn't fooled by the notion that a tie-dyed T-shirt was an expression of wisdom, and his argument—backed up by his glittering track record as someone who tried to kill himself with every known substance—that marijuana is the enticing entrance to needle park has yet to be answered. It was never invalidated just because Nancy Reagan said the same.

The Scandinavians, to do them credit, don't fool around with cosmeticized crime. Throughout the box set years, the Swedes, Danes, and Norwegians have done their best to keep crime ugly. Sarah Lund (Sofie Gråbøl), the head girl in *The Killing*, is not Mary-Louise Parker from any angle. Sarah Lund is a thin bundle of neuroses plunged into the gloom of a bad sweater. In *The Bridge*, the head girl Saga Norén (Sofia Helin) has a case of near-autistic something-or-other which would make any hetero male viewer think twice about angling for a lift in her Porsche, although it's probably true that any hetero male viewer would think of it once, because behind her unblinking stare she is very comely. At one point we see her having sex with her bemused bloke and she is under him, over him and off him in a matter of seconds, like the Scandinavian version of the female black widow spider, the one that carries a text book on how to form normal relationships.

And these head girls are just the cops. The criminals really get you down. Most of them are serial killers spreading terror in the standard Scandinavian ambience in which the lights are turned off even indoors, so that sometimes you have to search for the little green diode to make sure that your TV set is still on. Sarah, don't go into that stygian stairwell! You might shoot your partner accidentally! Oh. Even in the dark, however, it is made clear that a serial killer is a rare event, just as it is a rare event for someone to drop litter or travel without a ticket. This is Scandinavia, after all (it's all the one place: the bridge that joins Sweden and Denmark obviously joins everywhere else as well), and the scene is basically clean. Basically but not reassuringly. Far from it: under the cleanliness there is a current of angst, like someone weird softly reading aloud from Kierkegaard's *Fear and Trembling*.

And there is also the boredom. It is hard to get a job as a cop unless you are as boring as hell. (Saga is the *spectacular* Scandi cop because she not only stares at the wall, she occasionally stares at the wall for a long time.) I blame *Wallander*, who has been boring the world for so long by now that three different actors have played him if you count Kenneth Branagh. Of the two Swedish Wallanders, Rolf Lassgård tries to make the character interesting by looking around a lot, often approaching the looking-around record that Ben Kingsley established in *Species;* but the other, and by far preferable, Swedish Wallander, Krister Henriksson, accepts his northern destiny and just looks worried, like your dull cousin fretting about his tax return. Fretting away during the slow solution of a not very interesting crime, Henriksson's Wallander will stare out to sea as if wondering why Scandinavian waves are so small and dull. At such moments, which seem to last for hours, it is important to remember that elsewhere in the total Scandi crime-show effort important things are happening, especially when the story is about male evil on the loose, and what its resonance does to the female police who have to deal with it. It would be hard to imagine anything more consistently and legitimately frightening than the two episodes of the Swedish series *Arne Dahl* (it's the screen nom de plume of the writer Jan Arnald) that go under the collective name of *Mörketal*. Called *Hidden Numbers* in English, the two-part show is directed by Caroline Cowan, and for pace and atmospherics it deserves study, if only to remind you that there can be humanoid creatures far more horrible than vampires and zombies: people who look just like us, but whose humanity has failed to form.

Even at their least unexciting, however, Scandi crime shows seem designed to help you make sure that you won't be booking a flight in that direction, or indeed anywhere north of Paris. When the Americans remade *The Killing*, they turned the lights on and upgraded the heroine's sweater slightly so that you were merely incurious about it instead of incredulous; and in *Dexter* the serial killers get the benefit of a glittering Miami environment in which to lose the bodies. Dexter's neurotic sister Debra (Jennifer Carpenter) would be enough on her own to prove that nothing quite so glamorous happens with the Scandis even when they try, but even if she weren't there, Lucinda and I would have been transfixed by Dexter himself (Michael C. Hall), especially when he was transfixing his victims, although we sometimes turned to each other between episodes and wondered aloud if we might not have gone a bit strange. We agreed, after some discussion, that it was even more strange to buy one box after another of *The Following*, in which everyone is a serial killer except Kevin Bacon, but that it was worth it to watch James Purefoy (he who was such a bloody-minded Mark Antony in *Rome*) so credibly playing a psychopath.

That would be him, not us. On Lucinda's recommendation, indeed insistence, I joined her in watching *True Detective* throughout, as if I hadn't had enough, with the David Fincher movie *Zodiac*, of a couple of American guys taking so long to track down a serial killer that everybody including the audience grows old and gray. As an American serial killer serial, *True Detective* had the lights turned right up, even when on location deep in the Louisiana backwoods, but I could barely stand it: not for its horror, which is only about seven on the *Seven* scale, but for its main casting. It isn't their fault that I so dislike watching Woody Harrelson and Matthew McConaughey. Harrelson did good work in *Wag the Dog* and McConaughey in *Contact* was not really sufficient reason for Jodie Foster to flee the Earth: downbeat minor films such as *The Lincoln Lawyer* or *Killer Joe* have actually been held upright by his snarling, drawling energy. But add his face to Woody Harrelson's and you get a kind of reverse version of Butch and Sundance in which each seems bent on lowering further the spirits already lowered by the other. It was a relief when the extravagantly gorgeous Alexandra Daddario took her shirt off: the sequence, quite apart from its startling visual impact, had rarity value, because she has elsewhere always been careful to retain her clothing, to the extent, in her *Esquire*

shoot, of keeping her high heels on when she was half un-
derwater in a swimming pool. But a show is in trouble with
at least one viewer if it makes him search the screen in
order to avoid looking at the protagonists. How the viewer
reacts to a star's face is a deep subject, scarcely yet ex-
plored. (Farran Nehme has begun doing so in the U.S., and
Antonia Quirke in the U.K.: and good luck to them both,
because it is hard to say that anyone of any gender is more
attractive than anyone else without inviting a blog-storm
of excremental hatred.) All I know is that when I was very
young I couldn't watch Farley Granger in *Strangers on a
Train*, and that the aversion is somehow connected with
the feeling I have today that I would rather eat glass than
watch Nicolas Cage, even when he is being quite good in a
quite good movie like *Adaptation*. Such visceral, irrational
reactions are undoubtedly rooted in the deep, dimly lit
Scandinavia of the mind.

With Scandi politics, it's different from Scandi crime.
Though the level of lighting is still not high, *Borgen* seems
designed to get you running to the airport for a standby
flight to whichever of those double-glazed countries has
the greatest number of female politicians. The reason, dare

I say it, is that the central character, Birgitte Nyborg, is fascinating not just because of her situation—how can she keep her family life together while being prime minister?—but because she is played by an outstandingly disarming actress, Sidse Babett Knudsen. She needs to be disarming because Birgitte is living under a fearsome double pressure. (Really it's the same double pressure that Alicia is living under in *The Good Wife*, but Birgitte has got it in Swedish, so it's serious.) With the radiantly intelligent Knudsen in the picture, Birgitte's headquarters generates something of the same witty tempo as *The West Wing*. Her brilliant but twisted young adviser Kasper (Pilou Asbæk) could be Josh Lyman with his anxiety neurosis not yet diagnosed, and the media darling Katrine (Birgitte Hjort Sørensen) is a combination of Ainsley Hayes and Donna Moss, with enough teeth for both. Call the show *The North Wing* in conversation and people will know what you mean. It all sounds vaguely as if Aaron Sorkin had dictated it into a tape recorder while imitating a drunken German officer with a speech impediment, but one puts one's trust in the subtitles and tunes in for every episode, even after Birgitte, in the final season, falls from power. I'm bound to say that she suddenly then seemed much more ordinary, although the women in my family assure me that I'm a clear case of what Birgitte was up against all along.

What was she up against? Possibly it was residual male fear of female competence. Personally I can't get enough of being told what to do by powerful women, but I'm half dead. Back in the real world, women still must fight for a fair position. On the strength of the television output, we might tend to think they have a better chance of doing that in the European countries. Take a long look at the export-hit French cop show *Spiral* and you will notice that the head girl, Captain Laure Berthaud (Caroline Proust), can never stage a raid without the targeted culprit getting away through the back door, but that she is allowed to retain command of her squad of lumbering male dimwits. Meanwhile the beautiful female lawyer Joséphine Karlsson (Audrey Fleurot) pays few penalties for her gender: despite her corruptibility she goes on wowing the courtrooms like Alicia Florrick minus the scruples, while her equally smart male coeval Pierre Clément (Grégory Fitoussi) gets written out by gunfire. Sexual excess would have nailed him anyway: Laure and Joséphine both had their way with him. In *Spiral*, women are in the lead. It's a long way from the modern prototype of all French *policier* screen stories, *La Balance*, in which even the divine Nathalie Baye (be still, my foolish heart) was a helpless toy.

Is it fair to favor a pretty face? No, but it's life, and in fact the balance of evidence in screen history proves that a pretty face earns no automatic favor if it tries to say something funny. My late friend Christopher Hitchens was willfully wrong when he contended that women aren't funny: he was just generating controversy so that he could bathe in the uproar. There have always been funny women in real life, but on screen they were handicapped if they looked pretty, or even just normal. The Hollywood screwball comedy era, so formative for its stylistic boldness, had a swathe of wisecracking beauties, snappy with a line even if they didn't write it; but that temporary fashion died abruptly after World War II and was a long time returning to the big screen. On the small screen it looked as if it might never get started. As an admirer of Richard Benjamin (his 1982 movie *My Favorite Year*, which harked back to the formative television comedy years at 30 Rockefeller Center, set the mark for all the modern American screen comedy that I love best), I was as frustrated as he must have been that the comic talents of his wife, Paula Prentiss, were so often downrated simply because she was so fetching. Today, when I can spend hours watching boxes of *30 Rock*, I give thanks for all the fruitful groundbreaking that had to go on before there was a landscape that could contain Tina Fey: in all her work except for an oddly flimsy autobiography, one of her virtues is a capacity to honor the tradition from which she has emerged, and the *30 Rock* scenes in which Carrie Fisher plays a washed-up writer from earlier times are therefore touching as well as funny. But the biggest advance resides in the blessed fact that the power to decide these issues is no longer exclusively in the hands of men. The Hollywood screwball heroines could strut their enchanted stuff only because men thought the shtick would sell. Now, women are in on the thinking: they are in a position to take over the office and make Alec Baldwin entertain them, thereby giving him the best role of his life. In Britain, one of the threads of the wonderful all-women comedy show *Smack the Pony* was about how femininity and feminism linked up or failed to; and in America *Veep* cleverly (some of the cleverness is due to its British show-runner, Armando Iannucci) examines the pressures on an attractive woman of being a second-class citizen, i.e., of being vice president of the United States.

Veep would perhaps not seem quite so amusing if, in our heads, *The West Wing*'s absurdly superheated verbal atmosphere did not already exist to be spoofed, but nothing can detract from a sensationally authoritative central character: sensational at having no authority short of hysteria. The show's wildly funny star, the *Seinfeld* alumna Julia Louis-Dreyfus, is at the head of the picnic table in Amy Schumer's epic sketch *Last Fuckable Day* (permanently viral on YouTube), in which the assembled females, including Tina Fey, discuss the questions of youth, age, attractiveness, and the cruel dying of male desire. When the male viewer gets over his fits of guilty laughter, he might feel entitled to give himself a pass: how victimized are women now, if they can do this? For women it's been a long trail since *The Mary Tyler Moore Show*, but look at the trail now: it's a freeway. And comedy doesn't even look like a tough life any more, which used to feel like a decent reason for not being too sorry when women were kept out of it: male protectiveness, after all, is the acknowledged reason why women, though welcomed into the Israeli Defense Forces, are not allowed to fight in the front line. But however men turn the question over in their souls, women are likely to deal with it better on the screen: and I, speaking as a man, am glad not to be speaking at all when Tina Fey and Amy Poehler host the Golden Globes. Standing there cracking ten times as wise as Bob Hope ever dreamed of, each of them is backed up by a stack of box sets that few male headliners will ever equal. Seven seasons of *30 Rock* and five seasons of *Parks and Recreation:* how much of my time do these deprived people want?

No, the female performers of today are equipped with the power, as well as the impulse, to deal with the dialectics of their position. They would have slightly less freedom to do so if they were appearing on Al Jazeera, but by now most of them know that, and the point has almost ceased to be worth making; though as long as female writer-performers in some of the Islamic countries must go on risking their lives if they wish to speak freely, it will probably be worth remembering that Western civilization has some claim to its title. That television has been taking such an influential part in this great battle for equality is surely a cause to be thankful for having been alive in these times. The finally ineradicable conundrum, however, has to do with nature's casual cruelty in making some of us less desirable than others. Of all the bright and funny women who are now appearing in box set form, perhaps the most adventurous is Lena Dunham, because in her HBO series *Girls* she doesn't blink the fact that what separates her from the surrounding "sex goddesses" (her term) isn't a social construct, it's fate. It's what happens to you when, being a mere writer, and not especially amazing to look at, you would never make it as a character in the show you most worship, *Sex and the City*. Dunham's central bravery is to find a comic language for the battle against nature. Blake Lively of *Gossip Girl* never had to do that; and Lake Bell doesn't have to do it either, although she's funny anyway. But Lena feels that she has to do it; and, this being the twenty-first century, she does it, in a tongue that might seem effortless, but only to someone who doesn't remember what the twentieth century was like.

The Way We Weren't

IN THE SECOND DECADE of the twenty-first century, the twentieth century has already become a strange land, ripe to be looked back on through TV fiction. If you were there, the results often taste wrong, especially if they look right. A mental flavor is hard to re-create; but never mind, because you won't be around long to object. Trying to be generous as I bow out, I personally am careful to give points for any attempt at fidelity to the way we were, although all too often the flashback shows strike me as adding up to a startling registration of the way we weren't. What are these young people trying to achieve, when they pour so much money, talent, and effort into telling us what they think our lives used to be like? Well, if the first thing they strive for is a financial return on investment, they're certainly achieving that. And anyway, they'd do the same for Henry VIII: *The Tudors* and *Wolf Hall* between them must already have made more money than the dissolution of the monasteries. We should never forget that we're watching a market at work, even if the market is making the market the subject: self-reference is no guarantee of objectivity. It's more likely that objectivity had been made part of the pitch.

Among the growing worldwide audience for box sets of American television serials, the quiet but insidious craze for *Mad Men* spread at a highly sophisticated level. People latched on who would never buy a box set of *Entourage* (too silly) or *Californication* (too dirty) or *Band of Brothers* (too noisy) or *The Sopranos* (too grisly) or *The Wire* (too druggy) or even *The West Wing* (too witty). But a box of *Mad Men* they had to have, even if they hadn't seen a single episode on TV. Transmissions of *Mad Men* on mainstream channels, in fact, drew a notably restricted audience. In its land of origin the show was a hit for the cable channel (AMC) that developed it, but a big cable audience is a small percentage of a network audience, and in other countries the show was usually a minor event when it went to air. Even if it didn't rate on a terrestrial channel, however, the distributors of the box set were likely to get happy, because there was an upmarket consumer stratum out there whose hunger for the product seemed to be made all the sharper by the fact that hardly anybody else knew about it. It was like a taste for some homemade ice cream that gets taken up by a big manufacturer: the marketing will depend on the message that somehow the product is still home-made by Ben and Jerry, even though it's rolling out of a factory by the truckload.

There's a lesson there about advertising: a mass demand for something often begins when nobody knows about it except you and your friends. *Mad Men* is full of the les-sons that were learned about advertising in its late 1950s and early 1960s boom days on Madison Avenue. (*Mad Men* is shorthand for Madison Avenue men. But you already knew.) Because they were boom days, people came flood-ing into the business whose intelligence might previously have kept them out, and one of the continuing thrills of the show is the sense of mentally energetic people breaking fresh ground and building a new city whose ethical basis they might question if they didn't so much enjoy the law-less excitement, the sexy buzz, and the view from the top floors. In this respect, the show's closest predecessor is *Deadwood:* the Mad Men are ruthless Western desperadoes in tailored suits, swearing much less but smoking a lot more.

They, too, risk death. Indeed the actors playing the Mad Men might well be risking death from too many herbal cigarettes.

If the show has a weakness—and, dare I say it, it has— it lies in the fact that this thrill of contesting and tumultuous intelligence is too often damped down by a lingering emphasis on character. That could be part of the elitist appeal, however: when what sounds at first like a quick thriller by Raymond Chandler threatens to turn into a slow novel by Henry James, there will always be readers who feel flattered, and they might be right. Character studies are hard to do, and they give actors opportunities. The central figure of *Mad Men* is a character study and almost nothing but. Tall, handsome, enigmatic, and effortlessly dominant, Don Draper (Jon Hamm) is the creative genius of the Sterling Cooper agency. The agency's name is made up, and it turns out that Don Draper's name is made up too: or at any rate he stole it. During the Korean War he switched dog tags with a socially more privileged dying buddy and came home with a false identity. So he arrives on the Avenue with at least one interior conflict already working full blast, and there are plenty more waiting for him on the road ahead. His childhood, fragmentarily revealed in flashbacks—there is a storm of them in season 6—was hellish, and he can overcome it only by mass philandering: he betrays his current wife with his last wife and betrays both of them with someone else's wife. Don Draper is the most convincing portrait any size of screen has ever provided of a man compelled to begin his life again every few hours, each time with a new version of the only woman he can't do without. He's like Truffaut's *L'Homme qui aimait les femmes* with all the lightness removed and replaced with uranium ore. Today his career as a kinky mass seducer would be inhibited by the security demands of e-mail, mobile phone, and credit card account, but in those days a man like him could disappear at will, returning from a late lunch after manifold debauchery. His compulsive life is a refuge from his ruined childhood; his drinking is a refuge from his life; and buttoned up over all that turmoil is a fatally attractive cool-jazz façade. Bidding fair, unfairly fair, to being the single most magnetic male character of the whole box set era, Don Draper is Don Giovanni in a Brooks Brothers shirt.

The actor who plays him is ideal casting for a commanding figure racked by secrets. Blessed with a deep voice, an athlete's grace, and good looks beyond cavil but not beyond the bounds of credibility, Jon Hamm is the actor with everything, except the sense to change his name. There must have been a moment, just before he hit the big time, when he still had a chance to call himself, say, Jon Hunque. His agent and every friend he had must have been trying to tell him. "Listen Jon, for God's sake *listen*. You're going to be huge, but the word 'ham' means bad actor even with an extra 'm.' Change it. *Change it.*" But he didn't, because he didn't have to. We're in a new world now, when the mass market can cope with the raw facts.

In the old world, as represented in *Mad Men*, it can't. The facts have to be cooked, by the Mad Men. Few of the Mad Men are women, but since creative intelligence is at a premium, there is a door open for female Mad Persons to push through, even though the males waiting on the other side might have the sexual ethics of wolves fueled by alcohol. Doelike in her shyness of eye but needle-sharp in her originality of brain, Peggy Olson (Elisabeth Moss) is determined to break through a glass ceiling that is set at floor level. You loved her as Jed Bartlet's daughter: now see her fighting for *lebensraum* fifty years earlier. Made pregnant by one of the account executives—a marvelously off-putting performance by Vincent Kartheiser—Peggy hides the baby lest it slow her down. One of Don Draper's countless internal contradictions is that he can see Peggy's potential even while he continues to repress his wife without a qualm. Betty (January Jones) was a model, a Grace Kelly lookalike, until she met Don, but now she is a full-time housewife when not prostrate on the shrink's couch. She has no idea of what her husband does in the office, or indeed, away from the office after lunch. (The same applies for his second wife, Megan, played by Jessica Paré as an insecure beauty who has chosen exactly the wrong man to lean on: as Betty tells him when falling back into bed with him after she has married someone else, to be in love with him is the worst way of getting close to him.) When at work, however, even Draper must be on guard from detection by the all-seeing eye of office manager Joan Holloway (Christina Hendricks), she whose sumptuous behind is considered by the average journalist as the second most important character in the show. Most press pieces about *Mad Men*, especially if written by women, mention Joan's salient rear end even before they get around to the sexual challenge posed by Don Draper's brooding glance. The general assumption is that a dazzling job has been done of reproducing the way things were in those days.

It has, especially when it comes to things you can see. Right from the title sequence, which recalls the work that Saul Bass once did for Alfred Hitchcock, the look of the thing checks out in almost every detail. If you compare the look of the thing against the gallery of advertisements hilariously preserved on Lileks.com, it's a perfect match. The men's haircuts are exactly right, like their clothes. The women's clothes are so right that it aches: underneath, the foundation garments must be firmly in place. Everything graphic has been reproduced from scratch, thus avoiding the usual anomaly of art direction by which people in days gone by read old-looking magazines. Even those of us who were alive at the time will find it hard to find a fault, and those who weren't might well be led to believe that the atmosphere of a high-powered advertising agency has indeed been captured. Pulsing below ceilings that are almost always in shot—the camera spends half its time aimed up from below eye level—the pressure cooker is practically bursting with angst, ambition, and sexual tension. No hand-held shots; no Steadicam shots; even the technique is of the period. This, you are led to think, is the thing itself. But there is still more than one reason to worry about Joan's voluptuous figure.

She's a parody, and even at the time she would have been thought of as too much. Her early conviction that the only desirable destiny of an office girl is to become a married woman is very plausible, but her incarnation of oomph is a put-up job by the show's creator, who wants to give us a past much more clear-cut than it actually was. To give the show its due credit, as the seasons go on she climbs to power: a Mad Person possibly even brighter than Peggy. But she still never reads a book. Matthew Weiner—who is in control of *Mad Men* the way Aaron Sorkin was in control of *The West Wing*, except that Weiner has never allowed himself to be shaken loose from his creation—has devised a complex story about bright people, but he has simplified them while doing so. The concept that a woman should be a brood mare was certainly still prevalent, but men who were smart at the level of advertising executives had already begun to question it. When Marilyn Monroe swiveled her butt in *Niagara*, there were already plenty of men who knew it was a joke, and by the early 1960s the ideal of blatant sexiness had already given way to something far more subtle in the mind of any man who could read.

Right there, however, lies the biggest implausibility of the show. Most of the Mad Men carry on as if they read nothing except their own advertising copy. The only intellectual among them smokes a pipe, to indicate unusual thoughtfulness. The rest of them live in a world without books. Not even the supersmart Don Draper has a book in his house. At one point in the plot he stumbles on a collection of Frank O'Hara's poems and his brooding attention is captured by the printed word. (This episode has done for O'Hara's posthumous sales what *Four Weddings and a Funeral* did for W. H. Auden's, but this time the readers are probably doomed to confusion, because very few of O'Hara's poems get far beyond the condition of not being prose.) Draper also, at one point, dips into Dante's *Inferno*, no doubt finding a world ripe for market penetration. (I hasten to admit that I wish my own translation of the *Divine Comedy* had already been on the bookshop shelves when that episode went to air: I might have done a bit of market penetration on my own account.) At all other times, however, the agency's top ideas man behaves as if Gutenberg had never lived.

In *Mad Men*, the corporate world never questions its right to manipulate a captive audience. The truth of the matter was very different. Vance Packard had already published *The Hidden Persuaders*, and most of the people in the upper echelons of the consumer society had read it. Most of the Mad Men had read every issue of *Mad* magazine, a publication which, under the genial direction of its editor Harvey Kurtzman, was largely devoted to an unflinching linguistic analysis of salesmanship's bogus eloquence. Social critiques were best sellers, just as movies like *Marty* won Oscars. Bob Newhart, Mort Sahl, Tom Lehrer, Jonathan Winters, and Lenny Bruce had already made their satirical records and most of the Mad Men had heard them. At the time, Mad Men were part of the off-Broadway audience for Nichols and May. In the show, a bunch of Mad Men might get tickets for *Hair*, and Don and Megan might go to see *Rosemary's Baby*, but that's about it. In real time, some of the Mad Men—notably David Ogilvy—were already producing successful advertisements that parodied the assumptions of their own culture. Ogilvy's book *Ogilvy on Advertising* was a much-read *vade mecum* that helped the trade to consider itself as a profession precisely because its author emphasized the level of solid research and unpretentious practicality: "The customer is not a moron. She's your wife." Ogilvy's autobiography *Confessions of an Advertising Man* was—and remains, in my view—one of the key critical works of modern times. If the Mad Men couldn't

look like Ogilvy—he was as handsome as Don Draper—
then they certainly wanted to think like him. Armed with
their readings of books like his, and eager to emulate his
general taste and cultural hunger, the Mad Men were much
more conscious of what they were involved in than the
show makes them out to have been. They would have talked
about it among themselves. There would have been subver-
sive critiques a lot more penetrating than anything spouted
by Peggy's bad choice of radical boyfriend, the least smart
rat in her rat-infested apartment. There would have been
disputes, and, these being intelligent people, they would
have been intelligent disputes about ethical purpose and
legitimate method.

And that would have been the truly interesting conflict
in the mind of Don Draper. In the show he spends a lot of
his time questioning himself, but hardly any of it questioning his job. But questioning his job would have been part
of his job, because one of the ways that advertising developed was by becoming more self-aware. Advertising was a
medium, and that was what all the media did, on their way
to generating the media world we live in now.

The media world we live in now has generated *Mad
Men,* and it's a high-end product, with a sure sense of the

smart audience that preferred to find it than be hit over the head with it. Even when they *were* hit over the head with it by an adroit international campaign of promotion, they were still convinced that they were finding it all by themselves. But what they were finding was yet another illusion, though a remarkably nuanced and fascinating one. The illusion was of a past when even the smartest people weren't quite as smart as us. There is still much talk in the press about how the secret of the show's appeal lies in nostalgia —nostalgia for a time when a man was a man, a woman shaped like an hourglass full of peach juice had no ambition except to stay at home and cook, and everyone smoked like a train with no thought of ever hitting the buffers. But the show does better than that. It doesn't make the mistake of presenting life on the Avenue as a fairground.

Indeed it's a prison, and young Peggy will have to fight her way out. But few of them will *think* their way out, and the awkward truth is that a lot of them, in reality, were already thinking. They just hadn't figured out what to do next, mainly because they were involved in a paradox: it was the wealth they produced that would give them the freedom to question their lives. Stuck with the same paradox, we revel in the opportunity to look back and patronize the clever for not being quite clever enough to be living now. *Mad Men* is a marketing campaign: what it sells is a sense of superiority, and it sells it brilliantly. Personally I still can't get enough of it. But then, I could never get enough of Rothman's King Size filters in the brand-new flip-top box.

Displays of Secrecy

IN THE YEARS that the Mad Men were perfecting their language, the Cold War was being fought. Eventually it was won, and therefore it could be treated as if it had never taken place. The bottom fell out of the market for espionage fiction, which had depended on the concept that national secrets were vital. John le Carré had nothing left to write about. When he had, movies and TV shows based on his books were artistic news, and some of them still look good in retrospect. *The Spy Who Came in from the Cold* was the best starring role Richard Burton ever had, and the BBC TV series *Tinker Tailor Soldier Spy* is still potent in box set form, with Alec Guinness showing the male actors of the future how to do an enigmatic smile: even Gary Oldman, who attempted a frozen face when starring in the movie remake, was Jim Carrey by comparison. It should also be mentioned that out of the several attempts at a Kim

Philby chronicle, the best from back then remains the best today. It's the 1977 Granada production *Philby, Burgess and Maclean*, with Anthony Bate and Derek Jacobi. Bate, playing Philby, was plausible at being plausible, and Jacobi, who went on to be a compulsory cast member of any spy story for about fifty years, has never been better than he was as Guy Burgess, although saddled by the all-too-faithful script with the problem that Burgess, in real life, used to conceal his secret role by stumbling into London pubs, ordering a round of drinks, shouting "This is on the KGB!" and then throwing up into his own lap.

But unlike Madison Ave, the Cold War, from the viewpoint of the show-runners, was a case of there being no future in the past; and in the twenty-first century there have so far been surprisingly few flashbacks to the age of Mutual Assured Destruction, perhaps partly because of a general assumption that it really *had* been MAD, unlike the Mad Men, who were the cold warriors that not only fought the battle but left a heritage: the market world that we live in now. Yet there is a lingering awareness among intelligent people that the nuclear face-off between the two superpowers was no less serious a business just because the rockets never flew, and that the espionage effort from either side had been almost as vital a matter as John le Carré, in his prose of portent, said it was.

This awareness is what gives a show like FX's espionage thriller *The Americans* its strange authority. The tale of a married couple of Soviet-born sleepers living in Washington in the 1980s, it puts a big investment into getting the period detail right. It would be a handicap having to wheel on so many vintage automobiles, but there is a freedom in being able to stage a clear-cut battle: the KGB versus the FBI. (This being homeland America, the CIA has no jurisdiction, and does not feature, even though it was an ex-CIA officer, Joe Weisberg, who conceived the series.) The Red Sleeper theme is an automatic winner, because secrets have to be kept and a lot of hiding has to be done. (Still well worth watching, the 1977 Don Siegel movie *Telefon,* the story of a whole bunch of widely scattered Soviet sleepers who went into action as human bombs when they heard a stanza from a Robert Frost poem on the phone, was the second-best movie Charles Bronson was ever in, after *The Magnificent Seven.* Almost forty years later, Angelina's truck-jumping epic *Salt* was living off the same plot.) On the point about the nail-biting tensions of a life of concealment, *The Americans* saddled itself with an unnecessary weakness right from the start. To accomplish their schedule of spying and assassinating, Elizabeth Jennings (Keri Russell) and her husband Philip (Matthew Rhys) have to do a great deal of identity alteration, much of it accomplished by the wearing of wigs. As anyone knows who has ever needed to wear a wig professionally, putting the thing on so that it looks plausible is a task comparable to putting toothpaste back into the tube, and some of the wigs in *The Americans* are already starting off as looking pretty implausible anyway. Also, there is no mention of a secret lockup elsewhere in the city limits. Therefore they are keeping their wigs, along with their guns and other items of professional kit, concealed in the family house. Somehow their children never find the stuff. As a father of two daughters, I found this deeply implausible. In real life, children find everything in the house. Try a stunt like that and the day would soon come when your children would show up at the breakfast table wearing wigs and carrying a gun each. In *The Americans* it has never happened, but I am still sold on the casting. Rhys is a good Welsh actor blessed with the rare gift of adaptable teeth, and Russell is impossible not to adore, especially when she is plotting to kill someone while subtly registering her anxieties about her growing attraction to capitalist values. If you need a beautiful fanatic teetering on the verge of doubt, she's the actress you are looking for. Just remember that the FBI will take a long time to find her. While the insidious couple rack up killings and wreak havoc, the leading FBI investigator Stan Beeman (Noah Emmerich) is living in the next house, and takes ages to catch on. Admittedly, when he comes to visit, he is never confronted by a couple of armed children wearing wigs, but he still might have tumbled sooner if not distracted elsewhere in his work. He is distracted by yet another Soviet operative, the insanely lovely triple agent Nina Sergeevna Krilova (Annet Mahendru): no gun, but she doesn't need one. She has a complete range of high-tab Western lingerie, in various items of which she floats from one side of the screen to the other, touching the air with perfume. Stan, himself a married man, succumbs.

Meanwhile Ronald Reagan burbles suavely on the soundtrack, in his real-life role as president. The show could have been a farrago but isn't, and through the three seasons I have so far seen it has come to deserve its eventual hundred percent rating on the review aggregation website Rotten Tomatoes. (This universally favorable critical reception might have helped inspire Spielberg and Hanks to team up with the Coen Brothers for the hit movie *Bridge of Spies* in 2015: as in days of yore, shadowy spies met in the mist on the Glienicke Brücke.) The secret of *The Americans* as a show, apart from the deadly secrets, lies in the interplay between married life and incipient nuclear war, two scenarios that each depend for any stability on the capacity to know what the other side is thinking. Show-runner Weisberg was probably putting it a bit high when he claimed that each is an analogy for the other, but the comparison seems valid enough when Philip and Elizabeth sweat under the pressure of how to tell their daughter, Paige, that she has been brought up as a rather special kind of American. The daughter is often the moral pivot in a box set drama, and all too often she is the irritating daughter. It's an American secret: no other culture has such irritating daughters.

The irritating daughter in *24* plunges us forward into our present century, where there are two whole new wars going on. One of them is the war between one part of the CIA and another: a war that began with *Three Days of the Condor* but has now, in our time, become not a novelty but a given, to the point where the *Bourne* franchise of movies is about nothing else. The other war is the war of the occasionally united CIA against various forces that believe in

Allah's mercy and will kill us if we don't do the same. These forces are often also at war with each other, but they are united in their overriding aim to kidnap the irritating daughter of *24*'s Jack Bauer, played by Kiefer Sutherland and his gritted teeth. He grits them while straining to decide whether he should torture his captured enemies a little bit or torture them a lot, but he grits them most when his irritating daughter Kim, played with an admirable semblance of unbearability by Elisha Cuthbert, is kidnapped. When one group of kidnappers is somehow induced to release her, she heads toward another group of kidnappers so she can be kidnapped again. (The kidnapped irritating daughter is a subset of the irritating daughter motif but does not apply to Zoe Bartlet in *The West Wing*, who was kidnapped but was not irritating.) Not merely because, as a father of girls, I regard the theme of the kidnapped daughter as too serious to fool with, I gave up on *24* early, having guessed—correctly, as it turned out—that it had been designed to impress Dick Cheney's wife. There was also the fact that it had been made to look trivial by the first season of *Homeland*.

None of us predicted that *Homeland*, after its huge initial impact, would itself be reduced to triviality in little more than a single season, although we should have. At first blush, the story had everything, including a supremely irritating daughter. But when the hero Sergeant Brody (Damian Lewis, carrying all his tall authority from *Band of Brothers*) came back to the U.S. from his tortured imprisonment in Afghanistan and slowly revealed himself as a convert to Islam programmed to stage a suicide bombing against the American leadership, even the most riveted viewers realized that this might be a neat variation on *The Manchurian Candidate* but that Brody, win or lose with his mission, would be either blown or blown up after carrying it out. He could therefore have only a limited future as a character. This having proved true, beautiful but bipolar CIA officer Carrie Mathison (Claire Danes) became the center of interest. CIA veteran sage Saul Berenson (Mandy Patinkin) did noble work in the wise-man tradition of Gandalf and Obi Wan Kenobi; Morena Baccarin as Brody's wife was less lethal but even more alluring than the shape-changing alien lizard she played in *V;* and Morgan Saylor as Dana, the transcendentally irritating daughter, coped with the carpet burns when she, too, dropped to her knees in Islamic prayer, perhaps opening the way for a second suicidal explosion somewhere down the line. But plotwise all depended on Carrie focusing her scrambled brains in the interests of national security and world peace. Claire Danes seized the acting challenge with knotted hands and tossing head. Through more seasons than seems possible she has been devouring the screen, looking into every corner of it while speaking compulsively even when she is supposed to be inconspicuous in a crowded Arab market, nodding her head to mean no, shaking her head to mean yes. By now she has to do it without me watching, but I know she will bravely continue. Last time I looked in by accident, Saul's gift for meaningful taciturnity—his essential verbal knack is to go on sounding wise no matter how wrong things have gone—had got him into bed with an elegant CIA female subordinate, but it wasn't Carrie. Though Carrie no longer works for the agency, nevertheless she was outside in the Arab market, still attempting to be unobtrusive by looking around like a Tourette's victim and shaking her head like a dervish.

Carrie is a bright operative but can never seem to grasp that the word "covert" is meant to mean they can't see you. To be persuasive on screen, the covert personality needs a capacity for cool. The arch exponent of this for our time is Kevin Spacey. In *The Usual Suspects* he had looked like

Kevin Spacey with a limp, but perhaps he was really Keyser Söze, criminal mastermind. In *K-Pax* he looked like Kevin Spacey with a distant stare and a phenomenal ability to chalk equations on a blackboard, but perhaps he was really from a faraway galaxy. So when he arrived in the leading role of *House of Cards,* he already had a solid track record of perhaps being someone else. He was immediately credible as a careerist politician because he didn't look like an actor: he never has. Most leading men have sculpted features. Spacey's features just happened, like a Rorschach blot.

In the BBC's original of the show, Ian Richardson looked and spoke exactly like an actor, and a classical leading man at that: the eagle's profile, the cultivated voice that projected itself to the gallery of the Old Vic even when he murmured. The British *House of Cards* is big in my family, but I'm the dissenting vote: no doubt crassly, I find Richardson too obviously Machiavellian, his female victims insufficiently alluring to attract his fatal attentions, and the rats too symbolic: they get a walk-on role once per episode, usually just after Francis Urquhart (Richardson) and his Lady Macbeth of a wife (Diane Fletcher) have revealed new depths to their combined malfeasance. The American version I found to be a smoother ride, and thus more convincing.

As Frank Underwood, the ruthless Democrat majority whip working his way to the top by all means however illegal, Spacey is mercifully not obliged, as Richardson was, to hum "The Ride of the Valkyries" as an indication that he is gripped by the will to power. Instead he is given an even more lavish supply of knowing asides in which to transmit to us the cynically principled thinking behind his evil. Add all these asides together and you would get a treatise comparable with *The Prince*, plus a long free lesson in what a great screen actor can do by seeming to interiorize his emotions when in close-up. If the scene has already made the point, Spacey will underline it with no more than a millimeter of raised eyebrow: and nil by mouth. (Bad actors try to attract attention to their mouths: good ones know that our attention is already there.) This economy of style in the central performance is one of the show's chief strengths. Another is the elegance of Robin Wright, in her role as Claire Underwood, Frank's wife. She starts off as passive-aggressive, escalates to active-aggressive, and finally soars into the range of aggressive-insane; and all the way up the scale her smooth cool is playing against her behavior and therefore helping to define it. If, like Lady Macbeth, she ended up jumping from the battlements, she would fly like a bird. For anyone who started following Robin Wright's performances with *The Princess Bride*—Claerwen, when very young, used to make me watch it until I, too, could recite Mandy Patinkin's thrilling speech in the role of Inigo Montoya, and "Prepare to die!" is still a code phrase for the two of us—this is the apex of her beauty, even though (or perhaps partly because) it is accelerated by the burning internal fire of psychopathy that she somehow manages to convey by a hard stare, or sometimes just by an unexpected silence. Above all, she treats other women like dirt.

She would have done the same to Zoe Barnes in the course of time. But Zoe ran out of time: the show's sole example of willfully declining to develop a potentially fruitful long story line. Usually the production team is terrific at keeping a theme going: witness the patient care with which the story of Freddy (Reg E. Cathey), African American proprietor of Frank's favorite morning hangout for a plate of ribs, is followed up all the way through a long friendship until the moment arrives when Frank, having found it useful to help the previously contented Freddy overextend himself, cuts him loose to fall back into the poverty from which he had spent his life fighting his way free. Of all the instances in the show of Frank wreaking destruction for the sake of expediency, this is probably the most revolting: even more so than his murder of his political cat's-paw Peter Russo (Corey Stoll). But those acts of destruction each complete a curve. Zoe is destroyed too early in her rise to power; although I must admit that I grieved over her departure partly because I had so exulted over her arrival. Not just because she was played by Kate Mara, Zoe was dazzling as she raced upward through her first steps as a Washington journalist. She was Bob Woodward in nicer underwear. Making herself useful to Frank's plans, she traded her help for tips on stories: a relationship physically confirmed when he seduced her. But it could be said that they seduced each other, and that Zoe herself carried a share of Frank's virulent opportunism. Perhaps, to the show-runners, that was the trouble with her character: she might as well have been Frank. She was stealing his evil thunder. If she had really equaled his malignant gift, however, she would never have made the mistake of standing closer than he did to the edge of the platform.

After the subway train converted the alluring Zoe to mincemeat, there was a chance that I might have stopped watching, but the other plots within the plot were just too strong to leave alone. The mark of a great show is that every leading character is your favorite character, and my favorite of favorites is Frank's aide de camp Doug Stamper, played by Michael Kelly in full grimness mode: a reformed alcoholic, this guy is never off the alert. The factotum, or enabler, is a strong role in any gangster plot: think of *The Borgias,* and Cesare's deadly lieutenant Micheletto (Sean Harris), always one step ahead of his boss with the necessary murder. But Doug is the perfect instrument: an expression in himself of Frank's will at its lethal worst. For American TV, for anybody's TV, this is amazing stuff. Indeed, the whole show feels like a realistic antidote to romanticism, right up to the moment when Frank becomes president, after which, in my view, an incurable decline set in. Previously, *House of Cards* was *The West Wing* dissolved in acid. Now, suddenly, it was *The West Wing* all over again. Having attained the top role, Frank began playing the part straight, because there was no other way to play it. To operate plausibly on the international stage, he had to do the best that was in him. He was Jed Bartlet reborn: just a bit tougher on his staff.

Probably this development, or antidevelopment, was unavoidable. Nobody can stand out as Machiavellian in a context where everybody is Machiavelli, which is essentially the situation that obtains in foreign policy. This contretemps, which left Frank looking disappointingly normal, was a reminder that Machiavelli himself, along with *The Prince*, also wrote the *Discourses on Livy*, and that the two great books add up to a subtle treatise on what politics is bound to be. Sound-bite amoral ideas such as "it is better to be feared than loved" are rare in its total texture. Really Machiavelli's ruthlessness, to the extent that it exists, is meant as a safeguard against sentimentality. What most impressed Machiavelli about the times he lived in was the spectacle of the *profeta disarmato*, the leader who falls from grace through lack of the power to protect himself. Even after having been racked by the Medici, Machiavelli spent little time recommending that a leader would have to be purely evil to prevail. That was Frank's idea. It seems to me quite possible, although I wish it weren't, that the wide acceptance for such a show in the Western countries might have something to do with a growing fear that in a battle against absolute evil a leader without an evil streak might get us killed. Such a fear is primitive; but one of the salient qualities of recent long-form television drama has been to employ the utmost sophistication to face us with the primitive; and to make us realize that civilization has barbarism for a bottom level. Strip away the upper level and you are looking at *Game of Thrones.*

Game of Depths

LIKE ANYBODY both adult and sane, I had no intention of watching *Game of Thrones*, even when the whole world was already talking about it. For one thing, it had swords; and I had already seen enough swords being wielded by Conan and Red Sonya. Swords don't have to be magic to bore you. Excalibur, after all, though it appears and disappears magically, is not a supernaturally endowed sword: Arthur still has to do the fighting. Excalibur doesn't do it for him. Nevertheless even a nonparanormal sword is a formula for tedium, because the loser rarely shows the appropriate reaction: sometimes he is transfixed, and stares pointedly ahead as if reading a bad script; but hardly ever does he fall in half. In Kurosawa's *Sanjuro* he gushes blood after coming second in a quick-draw competition, but such realism is rare.

Though I share the movie heritage of my generation

in retaining a soft spot for the intricate fencing matches in the Errol Flynn *Robin Hood* and the Stewart Granger *Scaramouche*, the fondness rather depends on those lightweight swords making a little hole instead of chopping off a limb. Usually an on-screen swordfight is just a stretch of choreography, dull even when frenzied: or else it gets you into abattoir territory like that scene in the last episode of the first season of *Rome* when Titus Pullo (Ray Stevenson, pioneering the buzz cut) converts eleven gladiators into ten times as many body parts. No, there is a sound reason for not starting to watch any epic with swords in it. And to read such an epic is not much better. Not even Dorothy Dunnett, who can write, can write an interesting sword; and George R. R. Martin, author of the books on which *Game of Thrones* is based, writes the kind of prose that can describe a sword hand-forged from a meteorite and make it less thrilling than a can opener. I knew this because I picked up one of his books and fell down shortly afterward, and I wasn't even ill that day.

For another thing, *Game of Thrones* had dragons: and I place a total embargo on dragons. I would almost rather have zombies. Bolstered with these and other relevant prejudices, I managed to ward off *Game of Thrones* for months.

Then a box of the first season somehow got into my house. It lay there unopened on the parlor table while I thought of further objections. For yet another thing, *Game of Thrones* had Sean Bean as a hero, when everybody knows that Sean Bean is meant to be a heavy, one who flexes his teeth and grits his jaw before being eliminated by Robert De Niro in *Ronin* or Harrison Ford in *Patriot Games*. Leave that box alone! You don't have to look at it! You're sick, and time is short! Lucinda showed no inclination to help me fight my way through the shrink-wrap. We were binge-watching *The Following* at the time and that seemed kid-stuff enough. But one afternoon when I was alone, I found myself taking a peep. Almost the first thing I saw was Sean Bean gritting his entire face and then there was a not especially stunning blonde princess caressing a couple of dragon eggs. Yet I kept on watching, even as I vowed to stop when the eggs hatched. What was the immediate appeal?

Undoubtedly it was the appeal of raw realism. Superficially bristling with every property of fantasy fiction up to and including cliff-crowning castles with pointed turrets, the show plunges you into a state where there is no state except the lawless interplay of violent power. The binding political symbol is brilliant: the Iron Throne, a chair of metal spikes that looks like hell to sit on. (It was forged from molten swords by a dragon's breath, but skip all that.) It is instantly established that nobody in King's Landing or anywhere else in the Seven Kingdoms can relax for a minute: especially not the man on the Iron Throne. As for the top woman of the realm, she is a beautiful expression of arbitrary terror, which is probably the first way to think about female beauty, if not the best.

In a cast list where almost everyone stands out, the evil queen Cersei Lannister stands out most among the women, for she combines shapely grace with limitless evil in just the right mixture to scare a man to death while rendering him helpless with desire. She is Kundry and Lilith, Lulu and Carmen. She is Proust's mother, who tormented him so much by willfully neglecting to climb the stairs to kiss him good night that he spent his entire life writing a long novel in revenge. Superbly equipped by the cold edges of her classically sculpted looks to incarnate the concept of a femme fatale, Lena Headey beams Cersei's radiant malevolence at such a depth into the viewer's mind that she reawakens a formative disturbance. Did my mother look after me because she loved me, or was she doing all that only because she had to?

Plotwise, Cersei can thus raise a long-running question: must she behave dreadfully in order to protect her dreadful son Joffrey, or is she just dreadful anyway? Would we, in the same position, be sufficiently dreadful to protect our offspring from a richly deserved oblivion? Tussling with such conundrums, we are obviously a long way below the level of the law: and indeed the whole thrust of the show is to give us a world in which the law has not yet formed, a Jurassic Park which has not yet given birth to its keepers. Once this principle is grasped, the dragons almost fit, although personally I could have done without them. Lucinda, when I finally forced her at gunpoint to start watching, correctly told me to stop bitching about the dragons: they were part of the deal, the price of lowering oneself voluntarily into the pit of the brain.

The dragons hatch and grow up in the rocky realm of Essos, in my view the second-dullest region of the show's world-girdling range of locations. (The Seven Kingdoms are divided into nine regions, with a logic that will be familiar to all fans of fantasy, and even to a few normal people.) Sand is almost as boring as ice anyway, and when the sand is being trampled by an army of fearless gelding warriors, it induces sleep. Not that the Dothraki chieftain Khal

Drogo (Jason Momoa) is a gelding: *au contraire,* he looks like a pumped-up clone of the young Burt Reynolds, with the shoulders of an armored personnel carrier. Lover and spouse to Daenerys Targaryen (Emilia Clarke), she who would rule as many as possible of the Seven Kingdoms, Drogo is unbeatable, and unbeatability is always a formula for tedium. That same formula is at the heart of the currently most pervasive of all bad cinematic genres, the action movie without real action: where contending forces are invincible, there can be no plausible conflict, only choreography. At the side of the inconceivably butch Drogo, whom she tames by convincing him that his abrupt sex drive will yield even more satisfactory results if he extends the duration of the act of love to the full ten seconds, Daenerys can't lose. After all, she has dragons for an air force. She is not really the sex-bomb that the fan sites say. She is not much more than the average princess next door; but she has access to the only reliable supply of artificial fabrics in the Seven Kingdoms, and on her not especially maddening form a sheer negligee drapes wrinkle-free, like Ban-Lon on a Barbie Doll: the Hollywood concept of feminine allure always did depend on a certain insouciance about wearing nightwear by day. For all her putative capacity to drive strong men mad with longing, however, she is eventually obliged to look on helplessly as Drogo wastes away and dies, perhaps from boredom. If I sound dismissive, it's just because I'm still looking for all the reasons why it would have been right not to watch, before I get to the more difficult task of specifying the reasons why not watching would have been a loss.

Another reason not to watch would have been what happens in the North. There is icy cold instead of sandy heat, but still the level of tedium is very high, for two main reasons: the character of Jon Snow (Kit Harington) and the excessive number of CGI zombies. The latter component you can get in a bad movie. (Just lower the temperature of John Carpenter's *Ghosts of Mars* and you've got the whole Winterfell thing in a couple of hours, with no reason to watch at all apart from Natasha Henstridge in a teddy.) Continually assembling their forces to smash through the Wall and wreak who knows what havoc in the balmier lands of Westeros, the inexorably oncoming undead violate my ad hoc watching rule of never caring about any character that I can partly see through: I was brought up to be scared of people in one piece, not walking around in bits. But the real symbol of Winterfell's incurable problem is that Jon

Snow is no more expressive than the zombies. In this, I think, the casting has given us an ideal representative; for we, too, would be facially immobile at the prospect of forever defending a prop wall against an infinitude of implacable digital effects with no letup in the lack of interest. What you have to imagine is being trapped in a remake of *Assault on Precinct 13* with the set redressed as *Ice Station Zebra*. Or you could just stop watching.

At the risk of a spoiler, let it be said that the showrunners took a chance when they left it ambiguous about whether Jon Snow had been written out at the end of season 5. Nobody might have cared. His only accomplishment for several years had been to look glumly determined, even when the feisty Wilding Ygritte (Rose Leslie)—rather more fetching in her furs, let it be said, than any wispily clad princess from beyond the Narrow Sea—called him Jon Snore and shot him full of arrows. His in-depth moroseness is amusingly celebrated in a YouTube spoof video which has him sitting at a dinner party in New York and throwing a damper on the conversation, but really there is no criticism to be made of the character in either concept or performance, because the North of the show is simply like that: it leaves nothing to be said.

All the action that matters is in the intermediate regions, and especially in King's Landing, where the show begins and to which it must always return, if it has any sense. Luckily it usually does, and we know we will get back to it even when we are stuck outside in countryside somewhere with the towering Brienne of Tarth (Gwendoline Christie) endlessly escorting the tiny Arya Stark (Maisie Williams) from danger to safety, or from safety to danger, or whatever. King's Landing is Hamlet's Elsinore, Julio-Claudian Rome, *Deadwood*, *The West Wing*, and Tony Soprano's New Jersey all rolled into one. The other centers of events exist only to give us a rest from it, and the rest had better not be too long. This is where Sean Bean as Eddard "Ned" Stark, Warden of the North, newly appointed to be the King's Hand, graduates from his established condition of dispensability to the same indispensability that he enjoyed in *Sharp*, and then, while the old king slowly dies, goes on to a postgraduate degree as the wise man, the unwobbling pivot of the plot. And then what? He gets his head cut off at the mere whim of Cersei's frightful son, the boy king Joffrey.

Angelic to look at but talented enough to be anything, Jack Gleeson helps the writers give Joffrey a terrifying range of virulent psychopathy. ("They've killed him too quickly," I thought when the little swine finally got his, and I was all too aware that the script had reached me successfully in its clear intention to tap the viewer's animal emotions, some of which can have a disturbing connection with the way it takes so long for an orca to kill a seal.) But for the viewer who can stand back a bit from the kid's perverted smile, it's standard stuff. John Hurt as Caligula in *I, Claudius* ate the baby from his sister's womb, whereas all Joffrey does is shoot a few naked prostitutes with his crossbow. The real shock is not in what Joffrey's evil streak can accomplish but in what Ned Stark's virtue fails to prevent. He is a good, thoughtful man with a sense of justice; and it avails him nothing. It avails us nothing either, who have come to depend on him. For popular art, for any level of art, this is a rare step toward the natural condition of the world. The rarity might be multiplied by the unusual profligacy of sacrificing a star, but even that expensive boldness has been not unfamiliar since Hitchcock pioneered it in *Psycho:* as he told Truffaut, the shock value of Janet Leigh's early departure in the shower scene depended on the audience's expectation that a headline name would stay alive. But Sean Bean, though he might be admired, has never counted among the much loved, and the shock value of his departure from *Game of Thrones* depended on the size of the investment that the show-runners had put into building up his part of the story until it looked like the armature of the whole deal. For them, it was a key play in a deliberate campaign to get their show beyond the reach of movie cliché, and even beyond the reach of show business itself. Show business usually depends on fulfilling our wishes. In King's Landing, our wishes might run out of luck.

Cersei, for example, won't be climbing the stairs to kiss you goodnight, unless you happen to be her brother. She is more likely to consign you to sudden death. Since her every sardonic smile is a reign of terror, the script scarcely needs to spell out the secret of her political strength, but it's at its best when it does: one flaring illustration of how her mind works should be enough to convince any professional writer that *Game of Thrones* is a triumph of careful writing as well as of all the other aspects of production. (To be fair to George R. R. Martin and his Dan Brownish prose, the show-runners and chief writers David Benioff and D. B. Weiss have kept him close throughout the enterprise.) The suave and sinister palace tactician Lord Baelish (Aidan Gillen), walking in a courtyard with Cersei and her guards, for once pushes his flattering manner into the range of overfamiliarity. Quietly boasting about his treasury of secrets, he says, "Knowledge is power." Cersei orders her guards to seize him and cut his throat. They are all set to do so when she orders them to release him. Then she tells him: "*Power* is power." There are only a few scraps of dialogue in the forty seconds of the sequence, but it speaks volumes. It couldn't be done on the page with the same force, because you need the close-ups, especially of the fractured light in Baelish's eyes when he realizes that his own cleverness might have condemned him to death. The moment is a lesson in writing for the screen, and in *Game of Thrones* there are hundreds of moments like it. The show's long-running carbon arc burns between the extreme simplicity of primitive emotions and the extreme technical sophistication with which they are expressed.

An atmosphere in which a character as highly placed and clever as Baelish can talk himself to the brink of extinction with a single phrase really didn't need explicit scenes of sex and torture as well, but the show-runners piled them on: perhaps the global evidence that everyone with a brain was watching maddened them into the belief that everyone without a brain should be watching too. Personally, I could have done without the torture altogether. A scream from the other side of a closed door is usually enough to convince me. There is also the consideration that in the now-famous episode-long torture scene in the second episode of the third season, the actor doing the cutting up (Iwan Rheon in the role of Ramsay Snow) and the actor being cut up (Alfie Allen in the role of Theon Greyjoy) could, for my money, just as easily have swapped places. Rheon has the scarier pair of eyes—he can pop them at will—but Allen also looks like someone you would want to keep your eye on if he got behind you. In neither case can the actor be blamed for the face God gave him, but the whole dreary concentration on the sadistic delights of the dungeon was certainly the fault of the show-runners, whom we might have punished by ceasing to watch their show, if only we could have done so.

I can swear on a stack of Faith of the Seven sacred texts that it wasn't the sex scenes that kept me tuned in. In my clapped-out condition I didn't find their number and nature anything to be horrified about, but they were nothing to be excited about either. Though Lucinda yawned more often than I did, my breathing was not deep: merely lulled. Some of the female participants looked too gorgeous to be probable, but the same improbability occurs in everyday life, where chance dictates that you will sometimes see Venus Anadyomene at the supermarket checkout counter. There are Australian union officials who spend at least one night a week being thrown around in the middle of a nude beauty contest in a high-tab bordello, and all at the expense of their rank and file. The Saturnalian festivities in *Game of Thrones* struck me as a way of saying that in a prelegal society the higher whoredom would be an inescapable feature of life at any distance from the court and probably right inside it, if only in an upstairs chamber. The *Game of Thrones* revue-bar circuit has perhaps too many bare breasts and certainly too many Brazilian wax jobs, but there are no penises in sight: an indication that primitive times, like ancient times, adhere to Hollywood rules even when the starting gun fires for an all-out orgy. There is also the consideration that with so much compulsory removal of female clothes, an additional dignity is conferred to those females high-born enough to keep their clothes on, although this privilege, as always in show business, is mainly given to those who have graduated from the feature list to star billing. Thus we never see Cersei naked even when she is tumbling in the upper tower with her brother Jaime (Nikolaj Coster-Waldau), a scene which is therefore chiefly memorable not for her body laid bare but for the body of young Bran Stark (Isaac Hempstead Wright) lying broken after Jaime pushes him backward out of a window.

But if *Game of Thrones* actually depended on its torture festivals and showrooms of naked pulchritude, it would have been Gore Vidal's *Caligula*. The show's real spine is in the daring of its analytical psychology, much of it revealed through talk, which goes on even when the clothes have come off. (The word "sexposition" has entered the language; a clumsy coinage which I would never mention, except to illustrate the show's cultural influence.) Though economy is always the watchword, there are miles of dialogue, and nearly all of it is good. It's the reason why there was never a show harder to switch off once it had hooked you. You never knew, for example, what Tywin Lannister would say next.

For the deliciously long time that his character survived, Charles Dance never once chortled before he spoke, but he might well have done, for he was surely well aware that his lines were giving him the summation of his career in a single sweep. The overlord Tywin Lannister is not only the best role of its kind that he has ever had, it is the best role of its kind that anyone has ever had. (Rex Harrison got something as good in *Cleopatra*, but it didn't last a tenth as long.) The role gave Dance the delectable opportunity to play to his natural bent as an upmarket authority figure for four solid seasons, thereby stamping his image into the global public consciousness to a depth that his previous career had barely suggested. Had he accepted the role of James Bond when it was offered, things might have been otherwise; but as things were, he was lying around in fragments. Typecast as a smooth toff by his stature, looks, and finely cultivated voice, he had been perfectly at home in *The Jewel in the Crown*, *White Mischief*, and *Gosford Park*, but you were always wanting more of him. In *Game of Thrones* you get enough of him, and it still isn't enough. His role as Tywin Lannister has a polarity that he fits both ways. Tywin Lannister is a figure of authority, and that's just the ticket for an actor who elsewhere features in the video game *The Witcher 3: Wild Hunt* as the voice of Emhyr var Emreis, Emperor of Nilfgaard. But Tywin is also a philosopher of the subject of power, with his every precept learned first from experience and then refined by his understanding. And that's where Dance's greatest strength comes in: his credibility as a thinker, a man of reflection. There was never a more persuasively thoughtful transmitter of bitterly cured wisdom: in speech after speech he gets hours to do what Sean Connery gets only a few minutes to do in all those guru roles from *The Untouchables* through *The Hunt for Red October* to *Entrapment*. Tywin is wise from his mistakes, ruthless in his realism, an armed prophet after Machiavelli's own heart. For any male viewer he reaches deep into the psyche: we may not forgive him his cruelties, but we find it hard to question his right to rule. Look at the evidence. Nothing can stop him.

Nothing except the dwarf who shoots him with a crossbow while he is sitting in the privy. The dwarf in question is his son Tyrion, whom he has despised since the day the malformed boy was born, an instant reaction which finally turns out to have been Tywin's only long-term mistake. Peter Dinklage as Tyrion, from his first episodes in the show, had such an impact that he suddenly made all the other male actors in the world look too tall. It was a deserved success: his face is a remarkable instrument of expression over which he has complete professional control, and his voice is a thing of rare beauty, as rich as Chaliapin

singing Boris Godunov. But the compliments for his virtuosity must also go to the show-runners, who gave him the
opportunity to delight us with the range of his humanity.
None of his scenes really need to be cited in proof; everybody knows all of them too well; but if I measure his moments by my feelings, I have to recall his reactions when
he is on trial for his life in season 4, episode 6. His situation
is as desperate as when he must sleep in a cell whose fourth
wall opens onto a killing void, but here the threat to his life
is all in the words of others, and his resigned desperation, if
there can be such a thing, is conveyed not by the little he is
allowed to say—his summing-up speech is the only stretch
of eloquence Dinklage has been assigned in the whole trial
—but by what he looks like when he listens.

Debarred by fate from military prowess, Tyrion has
never been able to influence events except with his brain,
and his trial is the show's clearest proof that in an unreason-
able society to have reasoning power guarantees nothing
except the additional mental suffering that accrues when
circumstances remind you that you are powerless. Your only
privilege, even as a son of a noble house, is to understand
the fix you are in, and to express yourself neatly when neatness can avail you nothing. Tyrion has enough influence to

secure for himself, among his outsize supply of paid mis-
tresses, a woman he genuinely loves: the camp follower
Shae, touchingly played by Sibel Kekilli. But he can't save
her from harm; so even his best quality, his natural tender-
ness, becomes his enemy. Tyrion is the embodiment, in a
small body, of the show's prepolitical psychological range.
A perpetual victim of injustice, he has a sense of justice:
circumstances can't destroy his inner certainty that there
are such things as fairness, love, and truth. Those circumstances might lead him to despair, but he takes their measure by his instincts. Thus to raise, for an uninstructed audience, the question of what comes first, a civilized society
or an instinctive wish for civilization, can't be a bad effect
for an entertainment to have; although we might have to
be part of an instructed audience ourselves in order to find
that effect good, and we had better be protected by police
and an army from anyone who finds it trivial.

Philosophical conundrums aside, there is the matter of
Tyrion's indispensability: and here, surely, we finally come
down to a certainty that there is one character the show
can't do without. We have seen ourselves shocked when
Ned Stark gets decapitated, and we will be shocked again
when Tywin Lannister is killed by cross-bow bolts when

sitting in the privy. But we can survive those shocks, and might even have been able to bear it if the darling daughter Sansa Stark (Sophie Turner), after seasons of being protected like a caged nightingale even from the casual rapaciousness of the dreaded Joffrey, had been not only raped but killed, just as, in real life, some daughter equally precious is raped and killed every day of the week. Indeed, to put it as compassionately as I can, the dramatis personae consist largely of characters I wouldn't have minded seeing the back of. I liked the grim realism of Stannis Baratheon (Stephen Dillane), but, he being so realistic, how could he put up for another minute with the tedious scarlet woman Melisandre (Carice van Houten, bravely coping with the portentous dialogue of the numinous), the living, shape-changing embodiment of all I find hopelessly trivial about the occult? (Think how much less interesting Cersei would be if she were a shape-changer. Instead, all her deadliness falls within the range of normality. She is a smile-changer.) I also looked forward for far too long to the disappearance of the batso harridan Lady Lysa Arryn (Kate Dickie) down the same hole in the floor of the High Hall of the Eyrie into which she had precipitated so many of her enemies for a vertical trip of six hundred feet to the rocks below. (Our thanks here for a crucial assist from Lord Baelish.) Instances could be multiplied of those begging to be dispensed with.

Of those we come to love, there are many, but we have been ready to see them go. Young Arya, for example, braves so many fatal hazards with so tiny a sword that it would not have been surprising to see her pinned by her own toothpick like a cocktail sausage. Clearly the main thing keeping her alive was the determination of the show-runners to fascinate us with the process of her maturation, but from our own lives we know that the wish to see someone grow and thrive can be thwarted by chance. Everyone in the show is dispensable, as in the real world. But without Tyrion Lannister you would have to start the show again, because he is the epitome of the story's moral scope; and anyway he is us, bright enough to see the world's evil but not strong enough to change it. His big head is the symbol of his comprehension, and his little body the symbol of his incapacity to act upon it. For all his cleverness, there are times when only a quirk in the script can save him. Real life could kill the dwarf, but the show couldn't. So finally *Game of Thrones* stands revealed as a crowd pleaser. To despise that, you have to imagine you aren't part of the crowd. But you are: the lesson that the twentieth century should have taught all intellectuals. Now it is a different century, and they must go on being taught.

Ariadne's Labyrinth

THIS BOOK COULD GO ON for twice its length, but I think I have made the points that I was bound to make, and anyway I have not enough health left to do everything, much as I would like to. The concept of the superman is so deeply embedded into popular entertainment that one can easily be made to feel a failure for no longer being able to leap tall buildings with a single bound. But as we have seen with so many of the box sets, less corny concepts are increasingly likely to make their appearance on the little screen, even as the large screen becomes cornier than ever. At the very moment when Milla Jovovich, on the big screen, must carve her way invincibly through yet another busload of automata, the equally striking Julianna Margulies, still playing Alicia Florrick on the small screen, goes on with the much more difficult struggle for justice among human beings. She's an atheist, so she can't be president unless she lies; but as a pure soul plunged into the acid bath of the law she can be Princess America at her most complex, thoughtful, tender, and brave. *The Good Wife* isn't even a box set drama in the new sense. It's a television drama in the older sense of a CBS network weekly serial subject to cancellation season by season. It's still up there on television because the public loves it, and it's packed into boxes so that we can pay for it all over again. When the Microsoft CEO Steve Ballmer lost his position, he calmed himself down by binge-watching more than a hundred episodes of *The Good Wife*. I know something of how he felt. For nearly all the time I have been working on this book, Lucinda and I have been watching at least four episodes of that very show every Saturday afternoon. It's a reminder that in calling this recent upsurge of creativity a Golden Age of Television we have merely labeled part of an evolutionary process with an ad hoc descriptive term, an only slightly less than usually misleading specimen of the academic nomenclature that divides up the history of anything into manageable chunks. *The Good Wife* might have started going to air before there were boxes to fit it in, but it began with subtleties that later developments have not rendered obsolete, a fact underlined by the confidence with which it continues to deploy them.

There is a bad tendency among instant commentators on the media to suppose that all qualities began with the new wrinkle: but most of those qualities wouldn't have got there without being inherited from the old wrinkle. Luckily there is another brand of commentators, usually older and therefore less caught up in the evanescent glamour of the instant, who can reach back into their memories and point out that this business of continuously good writing throughout the long run of a show really began with *The Rockford Files*, and that a lot of what you love about Bradley Whitford unsuccessfully browbeating Janel Moloney was already there in the way James Garner talked sardonic rings around the hoodlums. Attractively incarnating a classic Dodge City sheriff redeployed as a U.S. marshal with the freedom to operate of a modern private eye, Timothy Olyphant in the excellent *Justified* would scarcely have a role to play if Jim Rockford had not first emerged from his trailer like Philip Marlowe with better taste in socks: not even the prodigiously creative Elmore Leonard, who supervised the expansion of *Justified* from its seed in one of his own short stories, could make up an entire tradition on his own, although sometimes when you watch *Get Shorty* again you might think he could. My wife, incidentally, *loves* Timothy Olyphant, but without *Justified* she might have had to discover him as the semiandroid star of that junk-channel staple movie *Hitman*, his fine head shining like a shrink-wrapped cantaloupe complete with bar code.

And so it goes on, from generation to generation: innovations remembered and developed, with very little that is entirely new, just as there are very few reactions in science that involve new elements, although occasionally, in the world of moving pictures, there will be one discovery, such as the invention of the close-up—the cinematic equivalent of discovering that plutonium had the right profile for neutron capture—that seems to change the game. But Rembrandt had already invented the close-up, and even he, however illustrious, was only one link in a long chain. In the cinematic story department, especially, the same rule applies that Richard Wilbur said was true for poetry: every revolution is a palace revolution. Nobody can be first: all you can be is the latest. To the credit of the many show-runners whose work is mentioned in this book, they know very well the long line of inheritance that leads up to them. For those of us with a less thorough practical knowledge, the past is nowadays being repackaged into box sets as if specifically to make us wise. Such a care for history is one of the undeniably good things about this marketing development. It serves the producer, but only because it serves the consumer first: capitalism the right way up.

Keeping the encouraging fact in mind that enlightenment is being furthered, we can safely note that Gresham's Law has not been magically repealed: badness will get in if it can, and any fad can become a threat. The box set concept has become so fashionable that a benchmark movie such as *Fargo* is refashioned as a series of television stories with the distant but certain intention of putting the stories into a box. The results are very good, but one quails to think of what they will be like when the same thing happens to *The Bridges of Madison County*. In France, the export success of *Spiral* was replicated with another police saga, *Braquo,* and this time there was no female captain to keep the male blunderers of the special squad in line, so they blundered even worse. The only female on the squad was in a subordinate position and contributed little except an unusually sour face, projecting, by French standards, an

almost Scandinavian sense of inner gloom. Without a female captain's guiding hand to make sure that the criminals
always escaped through the back door, the criminals could
now escape through the front door as well, while our boys
in the leather jackets and the three-day beards—all of them
looking like grunge chic models for *Vogue Hommes*—ran
in all the wrong directions. The show is so well directed
that you need eyes to go with your brains to see that it is
fundamentally dire, although not quite as dire as the long-
running Swedish police series *Beck,* which in Britain gets
the coveted double-episode slot on BBC 4 while *Braquo,*
for a first transmission, has to settle for a few thousand
people on Netflix. BBC 4 (the only indispensable British
channel, and therefore continually threatened with budget
cuts) screens two episodes of *Beck* back to back every Saturday night in exactly the same double slot that started off
occupied by *The Killing* but which you might have thought
had been made safe for France by the popularity of *Spiral.*

The obvious intention of the BBC 4 double slot is to
create the sensation of binge-watching within a restricted
time frame, and it sort of works if you believe that the lux-
ury of a long flight in first class can be reproduced by a
short-haul flight from LaGuardia to Cleveland. A few of

Braquo's episodes, by the way, are not entirely devoted to the usual struggle in French *policier* shows between bent cops we like and Internal Affairs cops we don't: occasionally the *mauvais garçons* turn out to be Islamic extremists, or anyway they are Serbians who know where the Islamic extremists are. In that way the most intractable problem faced by the French forces of law at least gets a mention. But on the whole, in the French police shows *pour l'exportation,* the way to deal with the question of militant Islam has been not to deal with it. Not long after I started watching the box set of *Braquo* I got the sense that its picture of criminal Paris, for all the horror of the torture scenes and the frantic, choppily edited action as the boys went booming around the *banlieues* in a BMW, was only pussyfooting toward reality. Then came the night of November 13, 2015, and suddenly the show looked obsolete, as if it was about nothing. But I shall go on watching, because it is so well made, and the subtitles make me feel cosmopolitan in a way that a few lines of Dothraki dialogue don't quite achieve.

On a world scale, so many new boxes are being generated that it's getting hard to keep up, but perhaps there is no need to fret. Something outstanding like *Catastrophe* will get plenty of media coverage: you don't have to find it by yourself. (Something isn't unfindable just because it's on Amazon Prime, although there are people who think that that's where Jimmy Hoffa is buried.) And anyway, the old boxes—I mean the prebox boxes, the shows that you once had to catch on the air if you were to stay up to speed—are available in sufficient numbers to keep you going until death and beyond. (What are the hard-core TV fans doing in eternity? They're watching the complete run of *Police Story,* so as to see how Michael Mann, though he was nominally only a writer on that show, might have begun working out his color scheme for *Miami Vice.* Then they watch *Miami Vice* again. Then they watch a dozen boxes of *Inspector Montalbano,* to find out what the police have been doing in Italy. Then they watch about ten years of *Kommissar Rex,* to find out what police dogs have been doing in Austria. Then they . . .) As we watch the older shows, I and both my daughters find that we notice more, because the new stuff has racked up our perceptions by a notch at least. In every chapter of *The Good Wife,* for example, you will find a neat treatment of some difficult theme that the average box set drama stretches out to a length that can easily seem indulgent. In the sixth season, Cary Agos (Matt Czuchry), after he is finally sprung from

unjust imprisonment, must further endure dreary questioning from dreary pretrial service supervisor Joy Grubick
(played with impeccable dreariness by Linda Lavin), con-
fidently exercising her duty to ask him obvious questions
and think a long time about his answers. Alicia also is
forced into the slow orbit of Joy Grubick and assumes, like
Cary, that the supervisor's painstakingly written opinion
will further the interests of the very bent, very bald state's
attorney James Castro (Michael Cerveris). But when the
crunch comes, it turns out that the dreary lady is the embodiment of true justice. This seemingly minor story line
demonstrates several of the show's favorite themes all at
once. It demonstrates the theme that our bunch of glam-
orously quick-thinking lawyers can sometimes miss the
point simply through being so clever. It also demonstrates
the theme that a face is hard to read: from the way Lavin
plays her, you would swear that the supervisor was as pe-
dantically malicious as Robespierre, yet when she comes up
trumps you realize that the awkward pauses she induced in
her interrogations were not a cruel tactic, they were pauses
for thought.

What it doesn't demonstrate, however, is any clear answer to the viewer's permanently recurring question of

whether Alicia's firm should be taking money from a drug lord. Though Cary is being framed, the prosecution's general case that our lawyers are profiting from illegality is true. Objections to the show's lofty neutrality on this point are probably just objections to the culture of the United States, but it's a big "just." Those of us in other countries can get used to the standard *Good Wife* office layout in which all the walls are glass: the door can shut on the sound of a conversation but not on the sight of the people having it, so everyone else in the office spends half their day wondering who among their colleagues and superiors is saying what to whom and why. This cultural quirk, a society reflected in its architecture, merely induces all the right tensions that are good for drama.

But for the loyally viewing foreigner it's a lot harder to accept that our favorite lawyer Alicia is being partly financed by the murderous drug lord Lemond Bishop (Mike Colter), although when a black actor plays a black hat it's presumably even better for community cohesion than if he plays a white hat: it must mean that at last there are enough black white hats, a long way to have come since the comparatively recent days—less long ago than the length of my lifetime—when Sidney Poitier was up there on his own, like Matt Damon on Mars. Besides, the show has plenty of nonwhite actors in sympathetic roles. From the politically correct angle, it's *The Love Boat* brought up to speed. Nor can you fault the show's attitude to gender equality and female fulfillment. As to gender, it has everything from the insatiably ambitious Diane Lockhart (Christine Baranski) right down to—or up to, if you prefer—the glitteringly gifted new hire Candace Frawley (Tonya Glanz), who clearly could go all the way but prefers to go home and raise a family. As to sexuality, it has Kalinda Sharma (Archie Panjabi), she of the big boots and the little legs, who keeps us, and half the characters whether male or female, erotically fascinated throughout the show: a vamp for all seasons, and it isn't even her fault. Her eyes were made for us to drown in, and for her to watch us struggle. (The rumor that she might be written out in season 6 induced global apprehension.) For the current generation of young women devoted to the show, watching Kalinda must be like their mothers reading *The Female Eunuch*, especially since lingering puritanical conventions of American show-biz dictate that even the multivalent Kalinda, along with the rest of the cast, can have sex only by suggestion. If it ever should occur that Peter Florrick (Chris Noth) resumes his wayward ways—at the time of writing the matter has been in doubt for six seasons—we can be certain that the female intern might lose her shirt, but that he will never lose his trousers.

If a Martian anthropologist arrived by flying saucer and set about investigating the sexuality of earthlings through reference to the American cinematic and television archive, he, she, or it would deduce that human copulation was something that takes place mainly in the kitchen, with the male pressing his trousers tightly against a presumably bare-bottomed female splayed on the kitchen counter, right there among the knives, cheese graters, and wineglasses still glistening with suds. Alicia and Will, however, are allowed to share a proper bed and some nice misty footage. There is always mist; although *The Good Wife*, to give due credit, has less of it than you might have expected when Alicia came wavering on stage in the first episode, still shattered by the revelation that her husband had found her less than enough. Julianna Margulies was built to walk on clouds, but the character she plays is down to earth, even to the extent that you sometimes wonder why she does not strangle her mother Veronica (Stockard Channing: a terrifying performance) or slap the face of her irritating daughter Grace, played by Makenzie Vega with an ineradicable teen sulk that deserves an Emmy of its own. (Young Grace goes missing in season 3, thereby transmuting herself from the category of Irritating Daughter to the even more nerve-wracking category of Possibly Kidnapped Daughter. Alicia copes.) But Alicia isn't perfect, even though she looks it. A hyperfeminist might say that an ordinary looking woman would have been more edifying in the role, but that would be like asking why, on the main French terrestrial channel TF1, the cool and graceful Carole Rousseau is the chosen anchor for six brain-curdling programmes about the no-go areas of Paris. It's to help make us feel cool and graceful, instead of desperate. Alicia is helping us to look at the unsettled and unsettling interface between the law and lawlessness, and if she weren't there we might not look. Fulfilling that task, she belongs to the world, even when saying things—"I haven't always been the best mom"—that could belong only to America.

But a good labyrinth is made from Ariadne's thread. It leads everywhere, and *The Good Wife* leads you not only back a bit into the network world that was there before cable, but forward into the galaxy of outlets that come next. Soon there will be no more box sets or even any DVDs, but the onrush of product will not be checked: on the contrary, it will be upgraded to a tumult that pours directly into the computer before your eyes, pending the day when the computer itself becomes an implant in your head. As Borges foresaw in his clairvoyant blindness, every library is a cyclotron. In the library of moving pictures, the continuity of the labyrinth is provided by the limitless mutability of themes and the limited supply of actors. There is a limited supply also of writers and producers, but that constraint doesn't show until things run thin. You don't have to travel through the cosmos of heavy viewing for very long, however, before you notice the same faces turning up. In Scandinavian TV they turn up straight away because in Scandinavia, wherever that is, there are only about ten actors, so fairly soon you will see a serial killer in one box set reborn as a detective in another. In Germany, Bruno Ganz is your only man to play the wise old chief of the antiterror squad. His face, weary with hard-won knowledge, confers automatic historic weight. But that's also what he's doing in *Downfall:* he's giving Hitler an upside. Ganz is everywhere because there's nobody else in his class. In the USA there are more actors than there are ordinary people in some small nations, but even in the vast population of American actors there are only a certain small percentage with the talent and the appearance to hold the screen. Below the salary level of big-screen stardom—the actors who are billed above the title—there is a general range of big-screen actors who are in constant demand because of the qualities they confer simply by appearing. As Anthony Lane has pointed out, anything is better if it has Stanley Tucci in it. Tucci does thoughtful decency. He also does thoughtful evil: moving into the area of box sets of old TV shows, you find him being villainous in *Murder One,* a show with an ancestral relationship to *The Good Wife.* The same relationship could be posited for *LA Law,* and, indeed, for *Perry Mason:* the connections of inheritance are endless. But there are only so many good actors to go around, so it is really no surprise that if you binge-watch the big boxes for long enough you will get familiar with what seems like a repertory company. Say goodbye to Dominic Chianese as Uncle Junior in *The Sopranos* and you may say hello to him as he appears behind the judge's bench in five episodes of *The Good Wife.* Watch the boxes long enough and you start wondering whether there will be a show based on the NFL in which Stockard Channing plays a linebacker for the Chicago Bears.

The show-runners try to cast for unfamiliarity, especially at the start of a new show: when *The Wire* got started, nobody had heard of Dominic West or Idris Elba, because they had received their thespian training in some faraway foreign land across the Narrow Sea. But inevitably, as time rolls on and you keep piling up the boxes, actors who belong in one box migrate into another. Sometimes you wish, on their behalf, that they could migrate back again. If Claire Danes in *Homeland* drives you crazier than her character, take a look at her in the TV show that launched her career, *My So-Called Life;* she was terrific, and you might be sorry that the show was canceled after nineteen episodes. But it's doubtful that she stayed sorry for long, because the cancelation left her free to be cast in Baz Luhrmann's film of *Romeo and Juliet,* in which she is a lyric poem all by herself.

Actors have to go with the market, which can be cruel. It is at its most cruel when it ignores you completely, but it can also be cruel when it doesn't. This book had its real beginnings in a winter when Lucinda and I sat down to watch *NYPD Blue* right through from the top for the second time in both our lives. More certainly than ever, Dennis

Franz's performance as Andy Sipowicz emerged as something monumental. The handsome guys in the show came and went: David Caruso, after finding out from the flameout of *Jade* that a movie career was not for him, recovered his stellar luster in *CSI Miami,* where he parlayed, into international recognizability, the art of standing sideways and putting on and taking off his dark glasses. Jimmy Smits arrived on his way to *The West Wing.* But for the twelve solid years that show-runner Steven Bochco's most startling creation was running, it was the balding overweight guy, Sipowicz, who was the living symbol of the show, a reformed alcoholic sweating in his short-sleeved shirt on a summer's day, suffering for his wayward son, breathless from unbelieving apprehension when he got the ideal woman. (ADA Sylvia Costas, as played by Sharon Lawrence, is a plausible candidate for an earlier incarnation of Alicia Florrick.) Dennis Franz's Sipowicz was a foundation performance in the Hall of Fame of modern American television. Yet afterward, when you saw Dennis Franz again, he was the airport cop yelling bad lines at Bruce Willis in *Die Hard 2.*

And that's the story of a *successful* actor. Sitting safely at home, we scarcely realize that these people are on parade in a slave market. We think of them as our property, and in a way they are; because the territory they inhabit has become incorporated into our mental landscape. Moving pictures are one of the main ways that the world is transmitted to us. We need to remember, though, that the very best they can do is not to tell us outright lies about that reality. For the subtleties, we still need books. While writing this book I was still reading half the day before I watched at night, and without what I read I would soon have lost touch with the nuances that matter. Only a third of the way into Rohinton Mistry's novel *A Fine Balance*, it became chasteningly clear to me why the screens could never tell me enough. The book is about poverty, and you might get something about a brave mother and her clever son from a movie or a TV show, but not even the memories of your own life can give you what the book does, because this is poverty of a different order. Reading about the sanitary arrangements in the Bombay slums, you quickly see why even the most realistic set dressing in *Game of Thrones* is essentially cosmetic. The imprisoned Tyrion may graphically complain about having been left to sit in his own shit, but you won't see it happen. How could you? It's only a TV show, and the TV shows, like the movies, are still camped in the dreamland that Elmer Rice made up for his 1930 novel *A Voyage to Puerilia* after he noticed that nobody on screen ever had to bother about the elimination of body waste.

A screen creation can't possibly give you the whole texture of the real: it can only strive to ensure that the picture it projects lends as little support as possible to the unreal. It is a dream that tries to hold back dreamland. Luckily the people in charge of *Game of Thrones* and the other big box sets have liberal values; and a national industry devoted to propagating illiberal values is quite hard to imagine, although Nazi Germany and the Soviet Union both had time to try before they died of their own beliefs, and in Egypt until quite recently the government-controlled television network was still screening a serialized drama based on that obscene old anti-Semitic forgery *The Protocols of the Elders of Zion*. Western intellectuals are quite fond of the idea that our systems of entertainment impose a repressive ideology, but really they impose nothing except a bewildering complexity. A Western intellectual stupid enough to envy the ideological simplicity of life in a culture whose ethics are controlled by theocrats ought to be locked up for as long as it takes him to laugh at an Egyptian television comedy series. For professional reasons I once had to sit through several episodes of one of these, and I thought at the time that if this was the product of the supposedly most liberal of the Arab nations, then one day we would be at war on a world scale. Eliot once spoke of the laceration of laughter at what ceases to amuse. He never had to experience the laceration of not laughing at what never begins to amuse; and we should take steps to ensure, by protecting our freedoms of expression, that our future generations never have to experience that either.

The long-form TV drama is the product of a free country. But the free country doesn't have to be America. Any free country can do its own equivalent of American cultural imperialism as long as it is willing to put creative investment into the part of the enterprise that matters most: the story. In that respect, everyone can take a tip from the Scandinavians. They had faith in their own gloom. It was like their faith that pickled herrings can be a tempting snack. Not once have the Scandis succumbed to the age-old assumption of the media organizations in the middle-sized nations that they can have an American-style success if they get themselves an American star. Combining their efforts, the British and Irish built their serial killer serial *The Fall* around the idea that their sexy female detective would wield more oomph if she was played by Gillian Anderson, whose career was established in the long-running American serial *The X-Files*. But casting her in *The Fall* looked less like a big-budget outlay than a confession of nervousness: it harked back to the postwar day when the British hauled in Brian Donlevy to pose as a scientific professor—looking and enunciating like a tough cop, as so many scientific professors do—in *The Quatermass Xperiment*. Enticingly impressive as the kind of implacable detective who looks ethereal in her underwear, Anderson, her to-die-for eyes looming large in the small frame of the BBC cameras, made local headlines in the kind of muffled casting coup that announces nothing except an insufficient budget to hire anybody more prominent. And although it was good to see that Jane Campion was willing to put her talented efforts into a long-form drama, New Zealand's export bid *Top of the Lake* lost a lot more than it gained by bringing in Elisabeth Moss to play its female detective. She showed all of the diffident fragility that had marked her performances in *The West Wing* and *Mad Men*, but in this role there was nothing more for her to show; and her glowing presence merely emphasized the pallor of the enterprise in all other respects, despite a very good-looking lake. In the same part, a local discovery might have laid the foundation of an international career. Alas, show business and pious wishes seldom go together. The massive global presence of the U.S. output distorts the force of gravity in any small nation's industry; and there was also the factor—so frequently decisive, yet so seldom acknowledged—of originality. For Jane Campion, the script was unusually recognizable. Privately I thought it was like *Twin Peaks* without the Log Lady, and I was soon in that cruelly indifferent state of not caring very much whether I missed an episode. Perhaps I had been spoiled long before by what the Americans could achieve by focusing their energies on the script without caring about exotic geography. If one of their cop shows is strong enough on the page, it doesn't matter if the New York precinct station has been rebuilt on a back lot in Los Angeles.

Working your way through all the boxes of *NYPD Blue* —a perfectly delightful occupation—you can watch the single-episode procedural story morphing into the overarching serial story of the complete season, and the seasons themselves becoming chapters in the total narrative arc: a developmental process which we can now, in retrospect, clearly see as the preparation for the box set drama. But prescience might have told us the same thing when we were watching *Shogun* back there in 1980. A maxi miniseries set in old Japan, it still looks new enough to make you wonder whether James Clavell, whose inspiration it was—he not only wrote the novel, he ran the whole gigantic production—might not have been the true founding father of the creative era that we have been considering in this book. *Shogun* not only has the fully working swords of *Game of Thrones*, it has the same violent terrors of a lawless society, except that they are exquisitely decorated with the kimonos and shy smile of Yôko Shimada. Even further back in television history, the show's leading man, Richard Chamberlain, put in five years playing Dr. Kildare, but as the English navigator working his way to power in an ambience bristling with bare blades, he looks forward to Ned Stark doing the same in Westeros. And the all-wise Shogun himself, as played by the great Toshirô Mifune, is the very prototype of the long line of wise men that culminates in Tywin Lannister. The Japanese have a special name for the wise man: he is the *genrô*, the principal elder. We may grieve that Charles Dance pronounced Tywin's last words, but we can be certain that we will see the principal elder yet again, under another actor's name; unless the tradition of the all-knowing sage was finally made untenable by Yoda in the *Star Wars* movies, backward his lines speaking in common sense defiance of.

I've only just remembered that Edward James Olmos, playing Admiral William Adama, commander of the endlessly fleeing space fleet in *Battlestar Galactica*, is a principal elder too. And I suppose Captain Jean-Luc Picard (Patrick Stewart) of *Star Trek: The Next Generation* is another; and Captain James Kirk of the original *Star Trek* also was, back in the innocent days of William Shatner's first hairpiece. (The Shatner hairpiece never really achieved warp speed until he starred in *T. J. Hooker.*) If SF were an inherently bad genre, like action comedy, I would have ignored it; but all too often it was full of ideas and invention, so I never could. I was already hooked years before I saw every episode of *The Invaders.* I was hooked in childhood by the movie serial *Flash Gordon Conquers the Universe,* starring Buster Crabbe as Flash and Charles Middleton as Ming the Merciless of Mongo. If I started remembering all the SF shows, however, I would end up making notes for a whole new book in which to discuss why big budgets and CGI effects have actually helped to diminish the genre, which is always at its most thought-provoking when the interstellar enemy looks exactly like us: the aliens in the *Alien* movies merely scare you, but the Cylons make you start counting your children. And if one of the aims of the average SF show was to attract an audience dumb enough to dress up as the characters, well, remember that one of the results was *Galaxy Quest*, a media-wise creation in the same league with *This Is Spinal Tap* and *Team America*. Alas, there is no room left to remember everything, and my own time as a wise man, if I ever was one, is nearly done.

Wise men everywhere, all over the galaxy, and far into the future! Will the wise women ever get their chance? But of course they will, and be wiser than us. As my image-soaked brain prepares for shutdown, of that much it can be certain: the television output of the Western nations might not be able to ensure, all on its own, that justice for women is secured, but it has already ensured that justice for women is encouraged and exemplified. The government of a free country could no longer get away with force-feeding suffragettes even if it wished to; public opinion, which is at least partly formed by television, wouldn't allow it; and anyway, free women have the vote. Protected against the worst of what men could do to them, women are at liberty to discuss what is done to them by nature. The TV shows are helping with that discussion all the time. When Alicia chooses to stay at work while Candace chooses to go home and have babies, that's a discussion; and when Hannah Horvath, preparing for the evening's battle against the sex goddesses, defiantly addresses the bathroom mirror ("The worst things you say are better than the best things they say"), that's a discussion squared, all taking place within the mind of one brilliant young woman. I never expected to see women get so far in my time. On screen, they are increasingly in good hands: their own. Lucille Ball started all that by making sure that she owned the sell-on rights to *I Love Lucy;* but it's still been a long slog, and Meryl Streep is only one of the many bright show business women who very properly remind us that it isn't over yet. But women, on screen at least, are a long way toward achieving a fair shake; and to the extent that they have not achieved it, they more and more have the chance of getting paid to say why. I just hope they find time to remember that some men were their friends: and that out there over the horizon, in the world that isn't free, there are still millions of men who sincerely think that the proper destiny of women who want to talk about these matters is to be burned alive or stoned to death, and preferably both at once.

But I wouldn't want to scare my ten-year-old grand-daughter by telling her that. I'm busy enough telling her that there are some scenes in *Friends* that are too old for her. She has a box set of all ten seasons, and I am allowed to watch along with her as she ploughs through the whole thing yet again. She doesn't seem even slightly fazed by the mentions of sex. I could wish that she were more both-ered by the laugh track, which is, in my professional expe-rience, a bad thing to have around even when comedy has been genuinely achieved: mechanical laughter is a false in-tensifier. But she seems to understand that instinctively, and brush it off. The next generation, and then the next gener-ation after that, are always more technically sophisticated than you expect, or can well credit. My granddaughter understands how Basil Fawlty gets his laughs. When Basil instructs Manuel to hide behind the reception desk, she knows that Basil is sure to forget Manuel is there, and will later on trip over him. When we watch the sushi bar scene in *Johnny English* yet again, she knows that Rowan Atkin-son is looking knowledgeable about Japanese food only to multiply the effect when he gets his tie caught in the conveyor belt. It is a language: the language of setup, structure, development, and fulfillment. It is one of the languages of imagination. She speaks it already. I took a long time to learn it, and soon I will speak it no more. But it will go on being spoken for as long as all these marvelous people are free to create. What a festival they have given us, and how hard it is to leave. I wish I knew a way to thank them all at once. Perhaps this little book might be a start.